❧ The Bridesmaid Guide ❧

⸨ The Bridesmaid Guide ⸩

Etiquette, Parties,

and

Being Fabulous

❋

By Kate Chynoweth

Illustrations by Neryl Walker

❋

CHRONICLE BOOKS
SAN FRANCISCO

Text copyright © 2002 by Kate Chynoweth.
Illustrations copyright © 2002 Neryl Walker.

Library of Congress Cataloging-in-Publication Data available.

ISBN: 0-8118-3300-3

Manufactured in China

Designed by Red Canoe, Caroline Kavanagh, and Deb Koch

Distributed in Canada by Raincoast Books
9050 Shaughnessy Street
Vancouver, British Columbia V6P 6E5

10 9 8 7 6 5 4 3

Chronicle Books LLC
85 Second Street
San Francisco, California 94105

www.chroniclebooks.com

Acknowledgments

Thanks to my editor, Mikyla Bruder, for her expert guidance and inspired ideas, as well as the fabulous team who helped this book come together, Jodi Davis, Karen O'Donnell Stein, and Vivien Sung.

Special appreciation goes to Sarah Putman Clegg, Erica Jacobs, Emily Miller, Alexis Scarborough, Rachel Scobie, Samantha Schoech, Wendy Sheanin, Jennifer Smith, and Lisa Taggart, whose wit and wisdom always cheer me up. To my mother, Judy Chynoweth, as well as Mary Bennion, Linda Peters, and Frances Verrinder, my gratitude for your support. Above all, thanks to Dave Griffith.

An extra word of thanks goes out to the savvy ladies who shared their inspired ideas and best bridesmaid stories: Christine Baer, Heather Belt, Lorene Bowers, Julie Blackwell, Lisa Campbell, Sarah Creighton-Kirley, Dana Donley, Kelly Duane, Christie Ellinger, Pamela Geismar, Lisa Gonzales, Julia B. Hand, Micaela Heekin, Christina Henry, Jane Hodges, Leslie Jonath, Allison Lengauer, Michelle Lutz, Leigh Morgan, Emily Russin, and Karen Silver. To the hundreds of women at parties, in bars, and on the street who shared with me their bridesmaid highs and lows, thank you!

Contents

The Shower and the Bachelorette 2

The Wedding Weekend **3**

Introduction

A bridesmaid, at her most fabulous, transcends the role of practical helper and friend to play an even more extraordinary role in the wedding— an unwavering bridge between the bride's old life and new. As only a best friend can, she remembers the bride's biggest achievements and most hilarious blunders, and she knows exactly how to celebrate the bride's past and future in style. She keeps the bridal parties rocking and the wedding good times rolling, for herself and everyone else. She protects the bride's secrets, and safeguards her own sanity. She's an excellent friend, and an essential component of every wedding-related event. Above all, she knows how to have fun!

Becoming a fabulous bridesmaid takes more than the simple commitment that friendship requires—it takes skills and savoir faire, and that's where this book comes in. We all have busy lives, and sometimes we need a little help and inspiration to be fabulous. We also need reminders of why it's so important to be there for the people we love on their big days. Packed with cool, surprising, and creative ideas for bridal showers and bachelorette bashes, plus practical tips for helpful bridesmaid behavior, this book will help you express your friendship in the way that suits you best.

In the first chapter, Being Fabulous, you'll get cozy and comfortable in your new bridesmaid role. With a breakdown of practical duties, etiquette advice, and budgeting tips, plus some astrology guidelines (for getting the scoop on what the bride's sign says about her wedding behavior), this is the overview nobody has time to give you. For ambitious bridesmaids who want to get creative, included is advice on doing the bride's wedding-day makeup and on getting certified to perform the wedding ceremony. Here are the guidelines you can follow to make yourself generally indispensible, mixed with plenty of inside bridesmaid jokes to help you maintain your sense of humor.

When it comes to throwing bridal parties, The Shower and the Bachelorette chapter offers everything you need to know. From classic etiquette and traditional events to wildly inventive party themes and games, creative inspiration for every hostess can be found here. Plus, a party-planning checklist, shower invitation etiquette tips, and guidelines for gift giving mean you can multitask and free time up for *your* life (things that aren't related to her wedding)! Maintaining your grace, humor, tact, and bank balance while throwing a bridal party is no small feat, but the advice in these pages makes it possible.

The final chapter, The Wedding Weekend, is all about staying cool in the spotlight, whether you're toasting the bride, taking a walk down the aisle, or twirling on the dance floor. The handy Groomsman Guide, and techniques for wedding-day damage control, will have you laughing all the way from the rehearsal dinner to the bouquet toss. Finally, you'll find inspired ideas for how to treat yourself right for a job well done—and remind the bride that you still care about her after the wedding spotlight dims.

Being a bridesmaid is about being a friend and helping the people you love through good times and bad. It's about being there for the bride in your full mind, body, and spirit—preferably, with a full cocktail in your hand. It's about living in the moment, and learning to laugh when you're wearing the worst dress of your life. Ultimately, being a bridesmaid is about finding creative ways to celebrate friendship—and it provides the perfect excuse to party with the girls. Amen to that.

Being Fabulous 1

THE GOLDEN RULES

The most important aspect of being a bridesmaid is finding that fun-loving attitude and bride-love within—so before we break down the old-fashioned etiquette and describe exactly what the job entails, you'll want to read up on these golden rules, the basic principles that every fabulous bridesmaid should live by.

Be Fabulous

Being fabulous means being loyal, enthusiastic, faithful, fun, gorgeous, and true. It is about being the best friend you can be. This has everything to do with attitude—feeling love and respect for the bride—and little to do with money or perfect attendance at the prewedding parties. (If you don't love and respect her on some level, think again about being her bridesmaid: if you have doubts in the beginning, just imagine how you'll feel after you've spent hundreds, hosted parties, and logged hours giving moral support.) When your love for the bride is alive, prewedding magic is afoot. Fulfilling your duties will come naturally, and you'll have fabulous fun while you're at it!

Know the Bride

Brides are as different from each other as snowflakes, and every bride will want different things from her bridesmaids. Use your knowledge of her personality to provide the kind of support she'll need. Does she have a particularly obnoxious mother-in-law-to-be? Run interference when the woman gets bossy. Is she concerned about finding the perfect gown? Tour the bridal boutiques by her side. As her friend, you have everything it takes to be the best bridesmaid around—especially if you are thoughtful enough to ask how you can help, instead of assuming you know her well enough to read her mind.

Have No Expectations

Getting married is overwhelming, and sometimes brides become neurotic versions of their former selves. Don't abandon her when she needs you most! Your emotional support and comic relief are the keys to her sanity. She may not be able to give back in the way she would under normal circumstances, but if you set aside your expectations—for example, that she should reward your efforts with formal thank-yous or gifts—you won't be disappointed. Cut her slack, often and always.

Bond, Girl!

Whether or not you already know the other bridesmaids, bond with them. You are all her dear friends, and she wants you to get along. Having a tight-knit group also makes planning and logistics easier for the bride. (Handing out copies of this book to all the maids is a wise contribution to wedding party harmony.) A well-bonded crew of helpful, fun, happy bridesmaids is every bride's dream come true.

Take Direction

The bride is your director, and together you are putting on a spectacular show—even if the wedding ceremony is simply a few close friends and family members gathered in an open field. This means that, for the most part, you should chuck your own opinions out the window. No matter how knowledgeable you are about weddings, do not make assumptions about what the bride wants. Don't assume that she is going to choose wedding colors just because you, your sister, or your other friend did. Think about *her*. Is she the type to know—or care—about such formalities? If not, you should not try to press any tradition, no matter how important in your opinion, upon her.

Fabulous Tip

How to Mix the Perfect Cosmo

Combine 4 parts vodka, 2 parts triple sec, 2 parts cranberry juice, and 1 part freshly squeezed lime juice. Shake well with ice, and serve in martini glasses with a wedge of lime.

Be Good to Yourself

Part of being fabulous is being true, and this means being true to yourself. Don't sacrifice anything too dear for the bride and her wedding, or you might end up resentful. If you can't spend four hundred dollars on the dress, tell her in advance, so the two of you can work it out. Also, don't get caught up in petty drama with other bridesmaids. Remember the big picture: You love the bride, she loves you, and weddings are celebrations of love and friendship!

THE NUTS AND BOLTS

Devised to familiarize you with the essentials of your new role, this section provides the bedrock foundation of knowledge you will need in order to survive—and thrive—as a bridesmaid.

THE BRIDESMAID'S OFFICIAL DUTIES

Behind every dazzling bride is an efficient crew of bridesmaids—the ladies who help the wedding love boat sail without snags—and you don't have to be an etiquette expert or super-sophisticated hostess to play this role perfectly. All that's required is that you be your most fun, funny, and fabulous self and take charge of a few basic tasks. With the help of a savvy maid of honor and bridesmaids who have their duties down, a bride can steer clear of choppy waters in the months before the wedding. The practical list on the following page includes the essential tasks every bridesmaid needs to complete to nail her job with creativity and class.

- Purchase the bridesmaid dress and shoes (without complaint), and be prepared to pay for professional makeup and hairstyling, unless you can adequately do your own.

- Be generous with your time and labor in the months before the wedding. Ask the bride if she would like your help with specific tasks, such as scouting for bridesmaids' dresses or stuffing invitations.

- Attend as many prewedding parties and events as possible.

- Help plan and cohost the wedding shower and bachelorette party. Contribute financially to these events and go in on group gifts.

- Provide constant emotional support and maintain your sense of humor.

- Arrange for your transportation to and from the wedding, and pay for your accommodations if necessary. Just because you are part of the wedding party, do not expect the bride to reserve or pay for your room and ride—these expenses are on your shoulders.

- Budget your gift-giving funds. In addition to buying a wedding present, you will most likely also give her gifts at the engagement party, bridal shower, and bachelorette festivities. How much should you spend? From least to most: bachelorette party, engagement party, bridal shower, wedding.

- Keep a record of gifts received at the showers so the bride and groom can write thank-yous. Collect any gift envelopes brought to the reception and keep them in a safe place.

- At the wedding reception, help bustle the bride's dress so she can cut a rug.

- The day of the ceremony, be there for the bride. Don't sneak off at any point, no matter how much you want to steal a private moment with the photographer's gorgeous assistant. The bride might need you.

- Attend the rehearsal dinner and ceremony. Stand in the receiving line after the wedding at the bride's request.

- Act as an auxiliary hostess at the reception by introducing people, directing them to the bar, or helping them find their table—but only if it seems necessary.

- Hit the dance floor with butt-shaking enthusiasm when the time comes,

even if nobody else is dancing. Don't be afraid that you'll make a fool of yourself. Dance with your designated usher if necessary—but in that situation, keep the butt shaking to a minimum.

- Be prepared to give a toast (or roast) at the rehearsal dinner or wedding. Technically, this is a maid-of-honor duty, but there are many occasions when it may be necessary, or just plain fun, for a bridesmaid to do the honors. How about having all the bridesmaids stand up together, taking turns reciting from the silly poem or speech you've written as a team? This takes the pressure off an individual speaker, and collaborating on the creative writing process can be loads of fun.

Maid of Honor: Extra Duties

When the bride asks you to play this part, she is sealing the deal on your lifelong friendship—but that fancy title and prestigious place near the altar does require a little extra work. Fortunately, the maid of honor is really about doing what comes naturally—being her closest confidante and empathetic listener, and, above all, being an energetic promoter of all things pro-bride. For a practical run-down of your duties, check The Bridesmaid's Official Duties list (above) and add these to your list:

- Attend one of the wedding-dress fittings with the bride.

- Make sure that all the bridesmaids have their dresses and accessories, that their hair and makeup is taken care of, that they get to the ceremony on time, and that they have the correct bouquets.

- Arrange the bride's train and veil before the ceremony begins and just after she arrives at the altar. Be prepared to help her "bustle the train" before the dancing begins. (This is why you have to go to the fittings—so you can learn the art of removing or shortening the train.)

- Hold the groom's wedding ring during the ceremony.

- Hold the bouquet while the couple exchange rings and vows.

- Dance with the best man during the formal first-dance sequence. Also, dance with the groomsmen, the groom, or anyone else who looks lonely for a partner.

- Help the bride change for her honeymoon, and take charge of her gown after the wedding-day events, arranging for storage in a safe place until she returns.

Word Alert

. . . .

❨ F O R M A L ❩

Yes, this word describes a high school prom, as well as a particular style of wedding—and, yes, the similarities are striking. Like proms, formal weddings are usually black tie, and they feature numerous wedding attendants, recalling the highly populated prom court. A formal wedding party will include at least six bridesmaids, plus a flower girl and a ring bearer. Semiformal ceremonies will be "black tie optional" and include fewer than six bridesmaids. Informal weddings will generally have an unspecified dress code and involve just a maid of honor. Dim lights, slow dancing, and public kissing likely at all of the above.

Top Ways to Form a Team with the Bridesmaids

When the bridal party is a tight group of girlhood friends who live in the same city or town, the bridesmaid bonding and group party planning happens naturally. When the bridesmaids hail from different parts of the country, however, breaking the ice between the girls is an essential first step toward making the prewedding festivities go off without a hitch. You don't have to wait for the bride or the maid of honor to formally introduce you—any bridesmaid can seize the bull by the horns. Use these tried-and-true techniques for getting the girls to bond.

You've Got Mail

E-mail isn't always the best tool for planning events—think about how easy it is to hit delete by mistake—but it is a great way to break the ice. Gather the addresses of the bridal party members from the bride and send an e-mail introducing yourself to the bridesmaids. Include some interesting facts about yourself (astrological sign, occupation, favorite cocktail), list your contact information, and generally talk up how much fun the wedding will be. Making a reference to the bride is helpful for reminding everyone that she is the common denominator. For example, if she has a reputation for being wild at parties, say something like, "Why do I have the feeling she'll out-party us all?" Encourage the bridesmaids to introduce themselves in a similar fashion by responding to your note. This works wonders for pre-party bonding!

The Buddy System

Pair up with another bridesmaid! Whether the task is planning the menu for the shower or buying some hot lingerie for the bride's bachelorette gift, chores are more fun done in tandem—and this will give you and your partner a great chance to get acquainted. If you don't feel comfortable assigning yourself a partner, ask the maid of honor to take charge of pairing you up to tackle certain tasks.

The Bride's Girl Friday

Every bride could use a personal assistant, and you can fill this need by printing an itinerary for the wedding day, or for any prewedding party. Providing a schedule that lists when and where the bridesmaids should show up will help things run smoothly, and if you print it on thick, pretty paper and tie it with ribbons, the list can be a lovely keepsake for the wedding album. For long-distance bridesmaids flying in a mere day before the wedding, this source of hard information will be a sanity saver—and sane bridesmaids are much more likely to be helpful and friendly than frazzled, crazy ladies.

Personal Contributions

Collaborate on a personal and creative gift for the bride—it doesn't even have to be anything expensive. Have the group write an irreverent song or poem dedicated to her. Get the ball rolling by writing the first segment yourself, circulating it via e-mail, and suggesting that the others contribute a creative line as well. You might also create a scrapbook, which could be sent sequentially to the bridesmaids, each of whom could contribute a story, anecdote, poem, or drawing before mailing it on to the next attendant on the list. (Allow a couple of weeks for mailing time.) Another lovely group gift is a charm bracelet—each bridesmaid can choose a charm and bring it with her to the wedding. When the bridal party gathers and presents the gift to the bride, each bridesmaid can explain why the charm she chose has special significance. Giving the bride a collaborative gift from all the bridesmaids will make her feel special, and organizing it in advance will give the bridesmaids something in common even before they all meet.

LONG-DISTANCE BRIDESMAIDS AND OTHER COMMON DILEMMAS

There is nothing conventional about being a bridesmaid these days, and things don't always go smoothly—but even the most awkward situations can be resolved when you communicate with honesty and tact. Whether the problem is having to fly across the country twice (for the bridal shower *and* the wedding), or figuring out how to cover that beloved tattoo revealed by the spaghetti-strap dress, these tips will help you navigate the most common rough spots with ease.

The Long-Distance Bridesmaid or Maid of Honor

Think of yourself as a version of Big Bird's friend Snuffleupagus on *Sesame Street*, the one who is always there when Big Bird needs him but mysteriously seems to miss all the parties. The fact is, the bride chose you knowing you live far away, and so she must feel that your long-distance emotional support is more important than your constant physical presence. However, some brides have unrealistic expectations, so if you know you cannot afford to fly out more than once, tell her in advance. With good communication and planning, any long-distance maid can be a lot more available than old Snuffleupagus.

If you are an out-of-town bridesmaid and think you can't afford to buy an additional plane ticket to attend a shower or bachelorette party, be frank with the bride early on, so that she has time to get accustomed to the idea. If she is really your friend, she won't begrudge your staying home. Be prepared, however: you may be asked by the maid of honor or other bridesmaids to contribute to the cost of the shower or bachelorette party even if you cannot attend. Etiquette does not require that you comply with the request, but if you can afford it, helping to foot the bill is a very generous gesture. If you're strapped for cash, there are many other ways to participate appropriately: sending a shower gift, planning a separate celebration with the bride when you do arrive in town, sending flowers, or contributing to a group gift are excellent alternatives.

Think about possible ways to maximize fun and minimize travel costs. For example, if you're planning a bachelorette party and all the bridesmaids live in the same town but the bride lives across the country, the bridesmaids can split the cost of the bride's plane ticket and fly her in for a weekend of fun. Be sure to plan far in advance, however, because a bride's schedule is tight in the months preceding her wedding.

If she's in Boston and you're in L.A., you can't always be there for her in person, but you can provide emotional support over the phone. Many brides treasure having an out-of-towner to talk to, someone who is far away from the hustle and bustle of their family and wedding plans, someone who has a sense of humor and a distanced perspective on the event. She may be too busy to call you, so take the initiative. Frequent no-pressure check-ins will let her know she's on your mind and give her a chance to vent.

If the bride likes the idea, you could fly in a few days before the wedding, so the two of you have a chance to do something special together before the final twenty-four-hour countdown begins. If you know in advance that you can arrive a day early, you might want to plan a luncheon or small party for the bride with the other bridesmaids. Find out what she's doing the day before the wedding. If it's a spa day, bring along a surprise bottle of bubbly and a basket of berries.

Two Maids of Honor

Think Thelma and Louise. Think Laverne and Shirley. Think what happens when the bride chooses two maids of honor instead of one! In fact, this practice is becoming more common, often because the bride wants both her sister and her best friend to stand up with her, or because she simply has two fabulous friends she cannot choose between. When this is the case, the two maids of honor split the duties between them.

If there is a particular duty you were looking forward to—holding the ring or signing the marriage license, for example—speak with the bride early on, but be flexible, of course. The maid of honor who lives closer to the bride may take on the more practical duties, such as hosting a shower or party, but both can equally share the financial, emotional, and practical obligations. Good communication is the key to avoiding tussles over this post's considerable duties.

Male Bridesmaid

Some brides may choose a fabulous male friend (a "bridesman") to be in her wedding party. His duties are essentially the same as those of any other bridesmaid—offering support and being part of the pro-bride team—although he may elect not to come to an all-female shower or bachelorette party. His wedding attire is the same as that of the other attendants of his sex (i.e., the groomsmen).

Pregnant, Tattooed, or Purple-Haired Bridesmaid

A pregnant bridesmaid was once considered to be in poor taste, but thankfully those days are over! Today, the bridesmaid's relationship to the bride is the pertinent matter, not her personal situation, and the only real concern should be whether or not the pregnant bridesmaid will be physically comfortable standing for the ceremony. Most brides will be flexible around other appearance-related issues, too. But if she asks you to modify your hair color or cover a beloved tattoo, only do so if you feel perfectly comfortable with the change. If not, and the bride insists on having her way, gracefully explain that this is a deal breaker for you—ideally, when presented with the prospect of losing you as a bridesmaid, she will think twice about her request. Although the bride's wishes should generally come first around her wedding, friendship is a two-way street, and all interactions should be marked by mutual respect.

RSVP Etiquette

Every wedding invitation should be answered in writing immediately, even when the bride has asked you to be her attendant and you have given your verbal consent. Also, don't burden the already overburdened bride with the details of your response, like the fact that you *think* your boyfriend is coming, if he can cancel his business trip, or that you want to RSVP for a tall, handsome man but you haven't met him yet.

Many wedding invitations these days include an engraved response card and stamped return envelope, which make the RSVP foolproof. These response cards are a recent development, however; in the old days, guests were expected to RSVP by hand, on their own stationery. This traditional approach is coming back into fashion, so you may receive an invitation that requires you to respond on your own steam. Here is how to do this and do it well:

If the RSVP is a blank notecard, you can reply by writing an abbreviated version of the text from the invitation, starting with your own name (and that of your significant other, if he or she is invited):

Sarah Putman and Sean Clegg

accept with pleasure

the kind invitation of

Mr. and Mrs. Miller

for Saturday, the twenty-sixth of June

at six o'clock

Wilshire Ebell Women's Club

If a wedding invitation does not include a response card but simply says *RSVP*, you should immediately answer by writing a response on your own stationery, in your own hand, following the form and language of the invitation, as above.

The List of Ultimate No-Nos

The road to hell is paved with good intentions, as they say, and that is truer for bridesmaids than for almost anyone else. Often because she has the bride's best interests at heart, a bridesmaid will overstep her bounds and unwittingly torment the bride. The worst part is that the bride may be too polite to mention the problem, in which case the poor bridesmaid will never know her error or understand why the bride seems slightly hostile. For the record, here is a list of the most common mistakes to avoid:

Repeatedly Asking the Bride about Wedding Details

You might think you're being thoughtful by asking the bride if she has chosen her "colors," sent out her invitations, selected the caterer, or completed other tasks—but, in all likelihood, you are tormenting her by reminding her of issues she has yet to resolve. If you must inquire, be sure you ask only once. She will bring her problems to you, if she wants to talk about them. (The fact that you did everything in a timely and orderly fashion is no reason to harass her.) Your job isn't to talk about the wedding; it's the opposite! Remind her that it's a big world out there, with lots of ridiculous things in it: tell her about the thong-sporting Betty you saw at the gym who fell off of her treadmill, or how you smiled at that cute guy and later realized you had poppy seeds in your teeth. Whatever you do, don't take your job so seriously that you start pressuring the bride. That's what wedding planners, mothers, and future in-laws are for.

Talking Constantly about Your Wedding Outfit

Some brides will want you to look *just so*—and you'll know when this is the case, because she'll prescribe not just the dress and shoes, but also your hair, makeup, accessories, and possibly even lingerie. Other brides will choose the basics and leave the rest to you, which means that she doesn't really care what lipstick shade, stocking hue, or hairstyle you select. Whatever breed of bride you've got, take the advice she gives and go with it, and if you need to consult someone, call a friend—one who isn't getting married.

Expressing Doubts about the Groom

Whether you mention that he isn't handling the caterer very well, or get down to brass tacks and say you don't respect him, making any insult to the groom is the cardinal sin of bridesmaid-hood. Yet the number of bridesmaids who make negative comments about the groom is shocking. The bachelorette party is the only time when you *might* mention one of his slightly galling traits, couched as good-natured ribbing—but only to provide contrast with his good looks, talents, smarts, and skills.

Expecting a Thank-You

You've worked hard throwing all the parties, and the bride hasn't breathed a word of thanks. What should you do? Get over it. Move past your own hurt feelings. The truth is, many brides are too overwhelmed in the moment to notice how hard you're working. She'll shower you with love later, when her head gets screwed back on—remember this whenever her self-absorption is shaking your faith in the friendship. She loves you, you love her, you're both fabulous, and there's nothing to worry about!

CREATIVITY RULES (WHAT CAN YOU DO FOR THE BRIDE BESIDES THROW PARTIES?)

If the couple in question loves to buck tradition or are paying for their own wedding (on a shoestring), your role as bridesmaid or maid of honor can take an intriguing turn. As a bridesmaid, you follow the bride's lead—and if she's a free spirit, you'll have carte blanche to be creative. Here's your chance to do more than throw bridal showers and bachelorette parties!

One of the most helpful things you can do is offer to take over some of the exorbitant but practical tasks that make weddings so profitable for caterers, florists, photographers, and stylists. Focus on your strengths. Do not, for example, offer to style her hair if you used to botch the job on your Barbies—but if you spent six months in cooking school, you might be the perfect person to bake her wedding cake. Not sure what to do? Try one of the following creative ideas! Not only will you save the bride money, you'll also show off your sassy, special talents and celebrate the depth of your friendship.

Perform the Marriage Ceremony

If the bride and groom aren't particularly religious and are planning a fun, freewheeling, and very casual ceremony, you can offer to be their officiant! Although the laws governing who can perform a legal marriage vary from state to state, in many places filling out the appropriate paperwork is all it takes for you to marry your friends. The state marriage-licensing bureau is the best place to ask for information; just be sure to get the wedding date right when you're completing the forms—your legal officiant status usually only lasts twenty-four hours. Alternatively, check for Web sites where anyone willing to fill out a quick form online can become a legally ordained minister—interfaith and nondenominational, of course. Be sure the state where the wedding will take place recognizes the type of officiant license you obtain, as the marriage must be legal to be binding.

Many couples adore taking this off-the-beaten path to the altar, since having a dear friend conduct the cere-mony can bring an intimacy that would otherwise be hard to achieve, especially with a justice of the peace or religious official who is a stranger to the bride and groom officiating at the wedding. If the couple choose to have you officiate, wear something that differs from the attire of the bride and groom and wedding party, although formal robes or vestments are certainly not required.

Make a Medieval Herbal Bridal Bouquet

Leave boring roses to the rest of the world and make her an old-fashioned and unforgettable herbal bouquet to carry down the aisle. Select a variety of gorgeous fresh herbs, such as lavender, rosemary in bloom, and flowering oregano—for a June wedding, these should be in season and easy to find—and surround the herbs with sweet-smelling peonies, preferably in pale lavender or other pastels. Wrap them with a sage-colored ribbon, and anchor all the stems firmly to create a bouquet sturdy enough to survive the bridal toss. (If you aren't sure about your bouquet-wrapping or flower-arranging skills, go to a florist with the herbs in hand and ask them to finesse the rest.)

Do the Bride's Wedding Day Makeup

If the bride is a close friend, the wedding is very casual, and you are a decent hand with a powder brush, you may offer to do her makeup. (Don't be offended if she opts for professionals instead!) Budget plenty of time and energy for doing the job if she accepts your offer—finding the right look will definitely take more than a quick trip to the drugstore. After all, you want to do it right! If this is your first time acting as a professional, here are a few guidelines to go by:

1 Several weeks before the wedding, book an appointment at the makeup counter of a posh department store that gives free consultations. Choose a product brand and corresponding makeup counter that fits the bride's budget—some lines are more affordable than others. Alternatively, book an appointment at a beauty product store like Sephora. (Sephora's selection is excellent, but their products don't come cheap.)

2 Go with the bride to the makeup appointment and watch the consultant like a hawk—if their products and techniques are making her look like something from *The Rocky Horror Picture Show*, drag her out of there. Never lose sight of the fact that you are in charge of quality control. Encourage her not to stray too far from her normal look. Resist consultants who give you the hard sell. You don't owe them anything, as long as they billed the service as free.

3 Book another appointment at another location. Continue this pattern until you find a consultant who does a reasonably good job of turning your dear friend into a blushing bride. Take careful note of the consultant's techniques before the bride purchases the beauty products. Professionals often use special tricks to create a certain look—tricks that amateur cosmeticians might not know about.

4 Once the bride makes her final color and item selections—with your gentle guidance—she should purchase the makeup, just as she would do if she had hired a professional. (Note: If you decide during this process that you and the bridesmaids should wear a lipstick that complements the bridal makeup palette, you should pay for that separately. Every bridesmaid is financially responsible for her own hair and makeup, in addition to her dress and shoes, unless the bride suggests otherwise.)

5 Do several test runs. Try the products on the bride for reactions or allergies. Look at the results of your makeover in the same light as that in which the ceremony will occur—in direct sunlight if the wedding will be held outside in the afternoon, and so on. If she doesn't like the look you've created, don't take it personally—just try again. On the day of the wedding, do everything exactly as you did in your rehearsals. Voilà! A lovely bride.

quiz

WHAT KIND OF BRIDESMAID ARE YOU?

Before the countdown to the wedding begins, take this quiz to assess how prepared you are for the challenges that await—think of it as doing a mock interview. Selecting your response to each of these sample scenarios will help you find out how naturally confident and fabulous you'll be in your new role. Knowing this early on should help you to troubleshoot accordingly.

You wake up the morning after the rehearsal dinner—the day of the wedding—with a strange man in your bed. He oddly resembles one of the ushers. . . . Oh, God.

a Think, "How will I live through this shame? I'm so embarrassed, I can't leave the room!"

b Grab whatever clothes you can find and flee, inadvertently locking yourself out and your bridesmaid dress in.

c Yell at him, "Get up and bring me croissants! I need sustenance before the bride and I storm the salon!"

You discover, mere hours before the ceremony is to begin, that the bridal bouquet has not been delivered and the florist can't bring it until the next day.

a ∤ Explain the snafu to the bride with hopeless tears in your eyes.

b ∤ Run like a maniac all over town even though you know there aren't any flower shops/they're closed/they're tacky, and arrive sweaty and late at the ceremony with a torn dress and no blooms.

c ∤ Pilfer flowers from vases at a nearby restaurant or the reception site, create the best bouquet possible, and offer it to the bride with a brave smile.

The formfitting dress makes you look more like you're carrying a wide load than like J.Lo.

a ∤ Blame yourself for not being slender or attractive enough.

b ∤ Tie a sweatshirt around your waist and forget to take it off before you walk down the aisle.

c ∤ Invest in some fabulous newfangled undergarments and make the best of it.

An ex-boyfriend, who is also a good friend of the couple, is shooting you very strange looks from across the reception room.

a ∤ Stare down at your plate, and as soon as possible escape to hide in the restroom.

b ∤ Gossip about him to your neighbor, ignoring the fact that the best man is in the middle of making a toast.

c ∤ Smile big at him and start picking your teeth in an exaggerated way. See how long it takes him to do a spinach check.

At wedding-day hair appointment, you notice the bride's hairstylist straying from the agreed-upon style.

a ⸱ Keep your mouth shut and leave it to the professional.

b ⸱ Focus so intently on your own hairstyle that you neglect to notice what's happening to hers.

c ⸱ Scream, "Oh God, her hair! What are you doing?!"

SCORING: 1 point for every a, 2 points for every b, and 3 points for every c

5–8 points ⸱ Fragile Bridesmaid

Unless you buck up, you won't be much help to the bride. Start on the road to wellness by being more honest with yourself and others and feeling more confident in your bridesmaid role. (Never be afraid to bust an incompetent hairdresser!) The bride chose you because she thought you might help her through this stressful time with style. Don't let her down.

8–12 points ⸱ Frazzled Bridesmaid

Your high energy level makes you an enthusiastic team player, but your tendency to act without thinking means that your attempts to be helpful may have the opposite effect. To avoid saddling the bride with more stress, find a relaxation technique that works for you—whether it's rubbing a lucky rabbit's foot or deep breathing—and practice it whenever you feel the overwhelming urge to jump in with both feet. You could even share your little mellowing technique with the bride. She probably needs it as much as you do!

12–15 points ⸱ Fabulous Bridesmaid

As a bridesmaid, you are funny, resilient, supportive, and resourceful. The bride is lucky to have you—but you knew that already! Your model behavior will inspire the bride and other bridesmaids, so be sure to offer them subtle encouragement to find the fabulous lady within. Most of all, enjoy all the unforgettable fun that follows wherever you lead.

YOUR BUDGET

Beware of hidden expenses! In the prewedding whirlwind of bridal showers, dress shopping, and parties, even the most budget-savvy bridesmaids can overspend by mistake. Because the events span several months, it can be easy to lose track of the big picture and splurge at each event.

THE BIG PICTURE

The figures listed here are meant to give you a ballpark idea of the financial burden that has fallen on your lovely little shoulders. But before you read on (and get ready to set fire to your savings), find the Budget Bridesmaid within. The Budget Bridesmaid feels righteous and good about celebrating a beloved friend's happiness, even if it means dropping some cash. At the same time, she cuts corners and shops for bargains whenever possible, and she has a clear idea about her spending parameters. Remember: Effective cost cutting does not make you a cheap person or a bad friend. It means that you are thoughtful and that you aren't willing to let money-related matters jeopardize your friendship with the bride.

The Dress (and Alterations): $150–$500

Cha-ching! The dress is *the* big-deal item for every Budget Bridesmaid. Your only hope is that the bride will not insist on something spendy—but no matter the price tag, you have little choice but to pony up. The cost of alterations, which can be upward of a hundred bucks, can also increase the overall price of the dress.

> ⸫ **SMART SAVINGS** ⸫
>
> If the dress is quite expensive, and so are your long-distance travel and lodging expenses, *and* the bride wants you to pay to have your hair and makeup professionally done on the day of the wedding, it is perfectly acceptable to ask her (in advance) if you can do your own beauty routine instead. She shouldn't mind your cutting corners in order to afford the dress, especially if she has chosen something on the high end.
>
> If you are lucky enough to be allowed to select your own dress, look everywhere from bargain basements to department-store sale racks to your close friends' closets. (Nobody has to know where you found the dress, or what you spent, besides you.) For a casual wedding, consider purchasing separates—they're easier to wear again. If you buy something brand-new, be sure it's returnable, in case the bride disagrees with your choice.

Shoes and Lingerie: $50–$200

We all live for fabulous shoes—and fabulous lingerie, for that matter—but when you need to cut costs, these are good places to skimp. Think twice about investing in pricey heels or bra and hose, unless special underwear is absolutely necessary to make you look and feel good in the dress. When it comes to shoes, consider the bargain-basement options before purchasing something expensive.

SMART SAVINGS

- If the bride frees you from the traditional dyed-pump route (around $50), hit the department-store sale racks or check out an affordable chain store and find something for $25 or less. If you've been requested to wear dyed pumps and you already have some from another wedding, you can re-dye them if the color is darker.

- Go for the cheap stick-on cups instead of an expensive strapless bra.

- Borrow that tummy-tucking thing from a good friend who shares your size.

- Go braless. Just remember that a chilly breeze at an outdoor wedding will make you the unexpected star of the show.

Hair, Makeup, and Accessories: $50–$150

The wide price range here accounts for the fact that the bride might want you to have your hair and makeup professionally done, which would obviously put you on the spendy end. Even if this is not required, however, you'll still shell out for wedding-day baubles and makeup, not to mention a manicure and pedicure. Sometimes, the bride asks all the bridesmaids to purchase matching accessories, in which case your hands are tied.

SMART SAVINGS

- Many brides give bridesmaids matching jewelry to be worn at the wedding, so if the bride doesn't give specific requirements, don't invest in new jewels—you may get some the day of the wedding. Bring backup baubles along, just in case the bride doesn't give jewelry.

- With jewelry, less is more if she doesn't give a mandate: Don't be afraid to go bare, bargain shop for accessories, or borrow your mother's pearls. Everyone will be too busy swooning over the bride to notice the details of your outfit.

- If she is not asking you to go the professional route, do your own hair, makeup, manicure, and pedicure.

Transportation and Lodging: $200–$1,000+

If you have to travel by plane, forget what you've heard about the dress being the most expensive item in the budget: when you add up the price of the plane ticket (or tickets, if you have to fly out once for the shower and once for the wedding) and accommodations, this cost definitely wins the prize as budget crasher. You are also responsible for arranging your own transportation from the airport to the wedding site, unless the bride offers you a ride.

⟨ SMART SAVINGS ⟩

- Plan ahead and shop around! Begin checking rates as soon as you have the wedding and shower dates, and make your reservations early to get the best deals possible.

- Team up with other single bridesmaids and share a hotel room—but do *not* let the midnight munchies persuade you to devour those expensive minibar snacks!

- If the wedding is in an area where house rentals are available, research the cost and see if you can drum up enough people to share a place—definitely the classiest and most civilized option for budget-conscious bridesmaids.

- If the bride has a friend who will put you up, by all means accept the offer, even if you don't know the person at all.

- Avoid having to rent a car by teaming up with local bridesmaids. If you must rent, try to coordinate with someone else to defray the cost.

An Individual Gift to the Couple: $50–$150

As a bridesmaid, you may already be in the red—and not just that scarlet strapless bridesmaid number, either—by the time the wedding day arrives. Luckily, etiquette is on your side: you have an entire year from the date of the ceremony to send the couple a gift, and delaying the purchase might give your bank balance a chance to bounce back. The fact that you are part of the wedding party does not mean your gift has to be lavish or expensive. Since you know the bride so well, you may bypass the registry and offer the couple something unique—something you've made yourself, for example—but don't feel compelled to do this. Buying from the registry is absolutely fine. Essentially, this gift is at your discretion.

- Go in with others on a truly fabulous gift. Just be sure to organize this effort with people you know reasonably well, and arrange the finances in advance, so you don't have to chase anyone down for money after the fact.

- Get crafty. Whether your talent is for painting, sewing, photography, or ceramics, use your skills to make them something priceless.

The Shower (Including Gift): $50–$200

The wide cost range for this event comes from the fact that you may have to share the cost of hosting the party. These days, it is common, and perfectly acceptable, for the maid of honor—who traditionally was responsible for footing the entire bill alone—to divide the financial burden among herself and the bridesmaids. Since none of the other guests at the shower should be asked for contributions, a long guest list might mean a large contribution from you. And, even if you help host, you should still bring a gift.

- Remember that shower gifts may be small. Elegant napkins, glassware, or other small household items are in keeping with the traditional intimate and tasteful shower, which these days is too frequently abandoned for a large party with lavish gifts.

- If you are attending more than one shower, you may elect to send the bride one significant item, rather than bringing a less expensive one to every shower.

- If you find out that all the bridesmaids are splitting the cost of the shower, try to get on the planning committee and offer a voice of reason if the budget

seems to be skyrocketing. Keep in mind, however, that bridesmaids should generally defer to the maid of honor.

- If you live far away and can't afford to fly out for the shower, you may gracefully decline the invitation. For further tips, see Long-Distance Bridesmaids and Other Common Dilemmas (page 20).

The Bachelorette (Including Gift): $25–$150

Since the cost of bachelorette festivities is nearly always split equally among the bridesmaids, chances are your share won't be excessive. For further savings, all the guests can contribute to a group gift as well as to the cost of the party.

⟨ SMART SAVINGS ⟩

○ Host a fabulous house party, so the budget for booze and food is fixed.

○ Feed the girls at home before you hit the town, so the entire group doesn't end up eating out at an expensive restaurant.

○ Select a gift that everyone can agree on, purchase it in advance, and have everyone split the cost.

○ Generally, the planning of this event is more democratic than that of the shower, so join the committee early and offer thoughtful budgetary cautions. As with the shower, though, the maid of honor often takes the lead.

○ If you live far away and can't afford to fly out for the party, you may gracefully decline the invitation. For further tips, see Long-Distance Bridesmaids and Other Common Dilemmas (page 20).

Total

At the low end, you are looking at spending hundreds of dollars. Now breathe deeply and remember that you love this girl, and that what goes around comes around. If you try all the Smart Savings ideas and still feel totally strapped, it's time to have a heart-to-heart with the bride, or get creative and cut the costs of parties and gifts with some serious DIY. Keep coming back to the worksheet opposite, and adjust the amounts as you receive information (use a pencil). You can't always control how much you'll have to spend, but at least you'll know how deep you're diving into the hole!

BUDGET WORKSHEET

Bridesmaid Responsibility	Estimate	Actual Cost (Write in Here)
The dress (and alterations)	$150–$500	$
Shoes and lingerie	$50–$200	$
Hair, makeup, and accessories	$50–$150	$
Transportation and lodging	$200–$1,000+	$
An individual gift to the couple	$50–$150	$
The shower (including gift)	$50–$200	$
The bachelorette (including gift)	$25–$150	$
TOTAL	$575–$2,350	$

Ten Signs the Bride Is Taking Her Bridal Magazines Too Seriously

Even the most practical-minded bride can be reduced to mush by the pressure cooker of the wedding industry. Watch for these signs that she's starting to lose it and take whatever steps are necessary to help her regain her wits.

1 She fires the sophisticated but practical caterers because they refuse to make Caramelized Duck Puffs with Cranberry Jewels at her request.

2 She fights with her fiancé because she wants him to wear gray-and-black striped trousers and an ascot, since "plain tuxedos are *soooo* last year."

3 She insists that the bridesmaids hand make crepe-paper peonies, complete with biologically accurate stamens and pistils, to wear in their hair on the day of the wedding.

4 She obsessively shops for a perfume to match the mood of her wedding (and demands that you accompany her on every shopping trip, since after the first sample she can't smell the difference).

6 She demands that the cake decorator make her six-tiered wedding cake replicate the pattern on her grandmother's eighteenth-century Wedgwood platter—even though it's broken into a thousand pieces.

5 She wants you and the other bridesmaids to create organza slipcovers tied with ribbons and festooned with fresh flowers for two hundred aluminum folding chairs.

7 She requests that you and the other bridesmaids purchase expensive matching seamless bodysuits to wear beneath your sheath dresses, saying, "No panty lines at my wedding!"

8 She is paying more than two thousand dollars for a miniature version of her dress for a doll the size of a telephone receiver.

9 Before she'll hire any officiant, she demands they take a Rorschach test.

10 She is botoxing her armpits—which involves lots of needles and thousands of dollars—so she won't sweat in her dress.

THE PALM PILOT

The maid of honor (or a local bridesmaid, if the maid of honor lives in another state or is otherwise engaged), in addition to hosting and attending the prewedding parties, has the responsibility of attending a variety of prewedding appointments with the bride. Use this schedule to forecast when duty might call.

AN APPOINTMENTS CHECKLIST

○ **Six Months to One Year Before the Wedding**
Help the bride shop for her wedding dress (and for the bridesmaids' dresses, if she so desires). This may entail visiting numerous bridal boutiques, both nearby and out of town. Free up your weekends. This can be time-consuming work, but it has the potential to be high-quality girl time.

○ **Two to Three Months Before the Wedding**
Attend the bride's dress fittings. Because you are her honor attendant, you should try to attend at least two. Ask the seamstress for tips on how to "bustle her train," if necessary. (These days, some gowns have trains attached with hooks and eyes or Velcro tape for easy removal.) You may also ask for tips on what product would best remove stains from the wedding-dress fabric—so you can keep a bottle handy on the wedding day. Always deferring to the bride, and her mother if she attends the fitting, offer your observations of the alterations as they happen. If an altered bust or waistline doesn't look right to you, gently express your opinion. Watch the bride closely and take your cues from her. If she looks like she wants you to say something, jump in there.

One Month to Six Weeks Before the Wedding

Attend her trial hair and makeup appointments. You know what looks good on her—and what doesn't—and if that dark eye shadow makes her look like a drag queen, say so.

One to Two Days Before the Wedding

Go for a manicure and pedicure with the bride. This is not a command performance, but an all-girl session at the salon is always a hoot. Plus, you probably need the grooming anyway to look good in your skimpy bridesmaid sandals.

The Day of the Wedding

Accompany the bride to her hair and makeup appointments, unless she feels more comfortable going alone.

WORD ALERT

. . . .

{ BUSTLE A TRAIN }

This might sound like a game you play with the cute little flower girl—*choo-choo!*—but it actually refers to the process of helping the bride get the train of her formal dress out of the way after the ceremony so she can hit the dance floor, and it is one of your bridesmaidly duties. Here are some of the train varieties that might be comin' 'round the mountain:

CATHEDRAL TRAIN: Detachable and three to six yards long

CHAPEL TRAIN: Detachable, very full, and eight to ten inches long

SWEEP TRAIN: Part of the dress; barely sweeps the floor

USAGE: The bride's mother says frantically, just before the dancing begins, "Can you help bustle her train?"

YOUR DRESS

A particularly thoughtful bride may consult her bridesmaids about the cost, color, and style of the bridesmaid
dresses—but it is common, and perfectly acceptable,
for the bride to choose and assign the dresses without
consulting you.

SURVIVAL STRATEGIES

With the dress often begins the torture: the exorbitant boxy pink suit that makes
you feel like a block of Spam and zeroes out your savings account; the strapless
red velvet minidress that might be more welcome at Hooters; the frilly taffeta
overstuffed-Barbie-doll number; the plain-Jane, high-waisted, six-year-old's
recital dress. Sadly, fashion tragedies happen at weddings all the time—and
you may very well be the victim of such misfortune. So how can you handle a
potential bridesmaid-dress catastrophe with grace and panache? Below are
some strategies for you to try.

Acceptance

The simplest survival strategy for dealing with an unflattering bridesmaid dress
is to graciously accept it: wear whatever and pay whatever the bride requests,
and keep your trap shut. Why? Because you love her, and being in her wedding
is more important to you than looking good.

Consulting the Bride

Another strategy that can minimize budget-related problems is to be clear
about your own financial parameters. To budget-challenged bridesmaids,
wearing an awful dress that costs a hundred bucks might be more acceptable
than wearing a pretty one that costs four times that much. Lots of bridesmaids
keep quiet on this subject for fear that sharing their financial limitations will
be seen as inappropriate—and sometimes it is—but, depending on the friendship,
having a heart-to-heart about money matters can be perfectly acceptable.
Discussing the situation early on, before the bride chooses the dresses, is the
best way to avoid resentments down the line. Once she has chosen the gowns,

any complaints on your part are bad form. While communicating your limited financial situation to the bride in the early stages is completely OK, you should understand that she might exclude you from the wedding party as a result. More generous brides might choose a less expensive gown or even offer to pay for it. If she foots the bill for your dress, bring this secret to the grave, so that the other bridesmaids don't feel slighted.

Tailoring

If you are unhappy with the fit of the dress, find a good seamstress. A talented tailor can do wonders to make that ill-fitting gown conform to your curves.

CHOOSING A DRESS

Some brides allow their bridesmaids to choose their own dresses, instead of assigning one that everyone must purchase. When this is the case, the bride may give general color guidelines, such as "pastels," or specify a color, such as "lilac."

There are a few unspoken rules that govern choosing your own dress. First of all, you don't have to tell anyone where you found it—so consider going through a friend's closet! Second, you don't have to tell anyone how much you spent. Finally, you should conduct your dress search without the bride's help (she probably gave you the responsibility so she could deal with other matters).

Sounds easy, right? It will be, as long as you have a few guidelines to shop by—without them, searching dress departments can feel like looking for a needle in a haystack. Beware the bride who gives you absolutely nothing to go on! In truth, most brides will have some idea of what your dress should look like and, at the very least, will know what they *don't* want you to wear. If she insists on saying, "Buy whatever you want," take it with a grain of salt, and try, through gentle questions, to nail her preferences down.

"Finally, an excuse to wear big, bold polka dots!"

This comment might give her a coronary, so only use it on a heart-healthy bride, and immediately point out that you're joking. Then ask her whether a subtle pattern on your dress would be welcome.

"I'm thinking about a dress with mutton sleeves."

This will get you talking style, the crucial factor in choosing a dress that will looks good next to hers. Does her dress have a high waist? A square neck? Princess sleeves? Flapper fringe? Find out the details and keep them in mind when you look at your options.

"Would you be OK with a supershort mini?"

This should make her laugh (if it doesn't, she's getting overwhelmed and probably needs a cocktail)—but the point is to find out how low your hemline should be. Does she want you to wear something ankle length? Is an above-the-knee skirt aboveboard? These are details you should know.

"Color Me Beautiful *says my best color is bright green.*"

Before she clears her throat and questions your sanity, reassure her that you only keep the book for laughs (and because your mother gave it to you). Then ask if she can give you any guidance on dress color.

THE BETTER BUST BRA CHART

Bridesmaids who forgo bras deserve a round of applause for their daring, but for those who require some lift—either because the strapless dress demands it or because you prefer support when performing for a crowd—here is the last word on what to buy for which dress.

Strapless or Off-the-Shoulder Dress

- **Bustier:** Surrounds the torso while pushing up the bosom; if the dress has a low-cut back or you have a voluptuous figure, a bustier is preferable to the more flimsy strapless bra.

- **Strapless bra:** Look for cups that lie flat against the ribs and be sure the back doesn't ride up. Advisable only for the small-chested bridesmaid.

Halter Dress

- **Bra with convertible straps:** Never heard of such a thing? Believe it. The straps wrap behind the neck and around the waist to prevent it from riding up and to keep the telltale signs hidden.

- **"Stay cups":** The cheap option! Yes, these are affixed to the body without straps (and, yes, they do resemble Tupperware and are advertised in women's magazines).

Sheath or Other Form-Fitting Dress

- **Seamless bodysuit:** Gives the smooth, sleek lines that this dress style demands. For more shaping and support, you can choose a stretch body dress that acts as both a slip and a bodysuit.

Other Tips

- Try your undergarments on under your dress in approximately the same light in which you will be standing—sunlight if the wedding will be held outdoors, and so on. Have a friend (preferably an honest one) look for visible panty lines or bra or underwear lace appearing through the dress material.

- Wear the undergarments out once, to make sure they don't chafe uncomfortably.

- Consider the potential weather. Will the ceremony be outside in the sun? No matter how much you like the idea of a seamless bodysuit, it won't be worth it if it makes you sweat like crazy. Go for a pair of simple body-shaping underwear instead—just remember to change out of those big beige underpants before you get some hot action.

Fabulous Tip

How to Avoid Offending Someone Important

When wedding strife strikes and key players are acting kooky, the urge to unload your opinion can be irresistible—but weddings are not the time to tell the bride what you **really** think. Confide in a taxi driver or a friend who will not be attending the wedding. Do a full visual check of all compass points before getting into the gab, to rule out the possibility of being overheard by someone involved with the wedding.

Tips for Happy toes

• If you are going the dyed-pumps route, be aware that they often shrink when dyed. Going up a half size when you purchase the shoes could save you from being hobbled on the dance floor. Better too big than too small, since you can always wear foot liners inside the shoes for extra padding and a closer fit.

• Often, brides will give general guidelines for purchasing shoes, such as "black strappy sandals." When this is the case, feel free to bargain shop, but don't buy cheap, uncomfortable shoes just to save money. As a bridesmaid, you may be on your feet for eight hours straight.

• Think about where you'll be walking—at an outdoor wedding on a grassy lawn, for example, wearing spike heels is not advisable.

• Whether you choose affordable or overpriced, simple or simply breathtaking, wear them around the house in the week preceding the wedding. Breaking in shoes on the dance floor is never pleasant.

ASTROBRIDE

Prepare for your job as bridesmaid by looking at her stars.

⁕ **The Aries Bride** March 21–April 19
The energetic, laugh-a-minute Ram bride will be a blast to work for—she'll generally keep her sense of humor and make sure those prewedding parties rock until dawn. But, be forewarned: her spontaneous, fiery nature means that she may change her mind at the last second about things you thought were written in stone.
Bridesmaid motto: Be prepared for anything.

⁕ **The Taurus Bride** April 20–May 20
Put away your glitter eye shadow: this classy, earthy lady has a healthy respect for tradition, and her wedding will be about simple elegance. She insists on high quality in every department, from classy gowns to gourmet food and drink. Lucky for you, you can count on the Bull bride to pick you a fabulous dress.
Bridesmaid motto: Put on the ritz.

⁕ **The Gemini Bride** May 21–June 21
A bride born under this mercurial sign will rarely take the traditional, well-trodden route to the altar, and her ceremony will be as creative and interesting as the guests. Ruled by the Twins, the Gemini bride may be indecisive when planning the details, so listen patiently to her myriad ideas and help her choose one path.
Bridesmaid motto: I am a rock.

⁕ **The Cancer Bride** June 22–July 22
The Crab bride prefers to lead—not be led—and will have very specific ideas about wedding details. She is very close to her mother and will want her to be involved in planning details. The slightest perceived criticism from a friend or mother-in-law-to-be will make the sensitive Cancerian retreat inside her shell. Encourage her to communicate her smallest concerns and troubleshoot when others act insensitively.
Bridesmaid motto: Don't worry; be happy.

⁕ **The Leo Bride** July 23–August 22
Don't get angry when this bride has moments of arrogance or vanity—she can't avoid them any more than she can deny her party-loving nature. Besides, few brides appreciate loyalty and faithfulness in friends as much as the mighty Lion. Be sure to plan a fabulous night out on the town with the ladies—with this bride at the helm, the bachelorette party will be an extraordinary and outstanding evening.
Bridesmaid motto: Keep your eyes on the bride.

✱ The Virgo Bride August 23–September 22

This perfectionist bride will tirelessly devote herself to planning the wedding, and you'd better be prompt at all the fittings, appointments, and prewedding events. What she really needs from you more than elaborate party planning is compassion and emotional support, despite her rather self-sufficient appearance. This bride can take care of the details, and your job is to provide the love—and loosening up—she needs in order to feel grounded and happy.

Bridesmaid motto: Be there with bells on.

✱ The Libra Bride September 23–October 23

Don't wait around for indecisive Libra, the sign of the balanced scales, to give you a color scheme or a to-do list. The fewer planning questions you ask her, the better—this classy lady will pull off an elegant wedding, but even she may not know how it happened. Spend your time planning a bridal shower or bachelorette party that will please her picky palate, but keep in mind that well-mannered Libra would be mortified if she thought you were spending more than you could afford.

Bridesmaid motto: Don't ask, don't tell.

✱ The Scorpio Bride October 24–November 21

Her wedding *means* more than most people's—at least that's how this intense bride perceives things. This bride can be a privacy freak, so you will be required to keep her secrets. At some point she may lose her tight emotional control and get wildly jealous about the groom's bachelor party or enraged at the careless caterers. Soothe her with her favorite sedative—a show of your love and loyalty. When the wedding day comes and this emotionally deep lady says her vows, there won't be a dry eye in the house.

Bridesmaid motto: Fasten your seat belt.

✱ The Sagittarius Bride November 22–December 21

She can be a little bossy, but will you ever have fun! From dress fittings to parties to the ceremony itself, the Archer bride will almost never lose her buoyant enthusiasm. Only when this extremely independent woman clashes with others over wedding plans will she get upset. The two of you might even squabble— but this girl never holds a grudge, and if you can forgive her in the same generous spirit, the wedding will be a laugh riot from start to finish.

Bridesmaid motto: Roll with the punches.

* **The Capricorn Bride** December 22–January 19
Your job—and it's a tough one—is to help this industrious bride put aside her perfectionist tendencies and have some fun! Surprise parties are a good idea, since she can't fret over them or try to do all the hard work herself. A Capricorn will rarely ask for what she needs, so plan lots of fabulous events that will distract her from fussy wedding details and appeal to her sense of humor. Family is very important to her, so make sure they approve of you; help them have fun at wedding events.
Bridesmaid motto: Forget perfection—let's party.

* **The Aquarius Bride** January 20–February 18
The Water Bearer bride has loads of friends—too many, you might think once you start trying to plan her bridal parties. Wildly gregarious, she tends to bond with people of every race, age, and gender, and she embraces their diverse preferences. She doesn't want anyone to feel left out. Be prepared to smooth over any social gaps that may crop up between her far-flung friends when they get together.
Bridesmaid motto: The more the merrier.

* **The Pisces Bride** February 19–March 20
This idealistic bride may be moody in the months before the wedding, feeling that the sacredness of love is being trampled by the wedding's endless, practical details. In fact, she might have eloped, except that her romantic streak can't resist a wedding. This sign is ruled by Neptune, the planet of illusion and fantasy—the very things that make weddings magical. She may search tirelessly for the perfect gown, but don't mistake this trait for materialism. In her heart, all she really cares about is that the emotional vibrations are right.
Bridesmaid motto: Feel the love.

The Shower and the Bachelorette

2

THE GOLDEN RULES

Planning the prewedding parties—the bridal shower and the bachelorette—is hands-down the most daunting part of being a bridesmaid or maid of honor. (If everything goes according to plan, these parties will only happen once in the bride's lifetime!) This section includes everything you need to succeed: scores of creative party themes, fun group games, and easy party favors, plus the essential etiquette for every occasion. But using these party-planning tips is only half of the equation. The real secret behind any fabulous bridal party is **attitude**. Let these golden rules be your trusted guide.

Personalize the Party

Not every bridal shower needs a menu of finger sandwiches and tea, nor should every bachelorette party include lewd drinking games or male strippers. Why? Because every bride is different. (Of course, if the bride has hinted she's always wanted to see a nude male revue, then you know what to do!) The thing to remember is that you *know* her—even if she was a childhood friend you've lost touch with recently—so use that knowledge to your advantage to plan an evening that celebrates her unique personality and tastes.

Never Assume Anything about Invitation Lists

Even though the bride has confided that she can't stand her fiancé's bossy sister—and you happen to dislike the woman, too—this doesn't mean you can leave her out of the bridal party loop. Weddings are not about whom you like, and they often aren't even about whom the bride likes. They're about family. So, yes, you may need to invite the bossy in-law to the shower, and to the bachelorette as well.

Be Firm (and Discreet) about the Budget

Talking about money during celebratory times can make you feel like Ebenezer Scrooge, but don't feel shy about communicating clearly with the maids about the cold, hard cash. Keep track of who contributed what, and solicit funds when necessary. Do not, however, discuss budgetary issues with the bride.

Remember Your Pecking Order

The maid of honor is in charge. Although she and the bridesmaids work as a team, the primary honor attendant should have the final say in any contentious decision. If she lives out of town and can only fly in for the wedding, a local bridesmaid might step in and fill her role during the prewedding festivities. It is helpful to have someone in charge of the troupe with so many decisions to be made, so whoever takes the wheel, respect her authority.

Get What You Pay For

If you and the other bridesmaids are hosting a party at a bar or restaurant that you're not completely familiar with, send a scout to sample the atmosphere, food, and drink. That way you can ensure that the spot is good and get a solid idea of the prices. The same goes for hiring "talent" for a party— don't just call any astrologer in the yellow pages, do the research to find someone fabulous.

THE BRIDAL SHOWER

Bridal showers can be small, intimate, and ladies only, or they can be big affairs that include the groom and his friends and family—but the main point is to honor the bride and "shower" her with gifts.

THE BIG PICTURE

When several people or different groups of friends want the honor of hosting a shower, the bride may receive more than one. The most traditional shower, however, is the one thrown by the maid of honor and bridesmaids, and this usually happens a month or more before the wedding. Since the guest list at this event includes the bride's mother and her classy, older crowd, many young hostesses have more than a touch of nerves over how formal to make the event.

Whether you are hosting alone or with the whole team of bridesmaids, and whether you are inviting eight people or eighty, remember one simple fact: a bridal shower is an opportunity to celebrate the bride and her upcoming nuptials, not to prove yourself as a master chef or crack party planner. Don't feel pressured by the fact that parental types will be there, and don't feel compelled to behave like Martha Stewart if that is not your usual MO. With a little careful planning, and lots of bride-love, any shower can be a big hit!

This overview of bridal shower protocol puts important information at your fingertips. When you follow these etiquette tips, even the bride's most proper relatives will find your party—and its planning process—gracious and charming.

Hosting Duties

Traditionally, the maid of honor is in charge. If she lives far away or is otherwise unavailable, any bridesmaid, coworker, or member of the bride's extended family, such as an aunt or cousin, may do the honors. (According to etiquette, immediate members of the bride's family, such as her mother or sister, should *not* host, since it may seem like an obvious bid for booty.) In today's world of long-distance friendships and relaxed etiquette rules, hosting a bridal shower is defined less by your role in the bride's wedding than by your proximity to the bride and her family, and your willingness to play hostess.

Money Matters

The hostess underwrites the party. If the maid of honor hosts, it is perfectly acceptable for her to ask the bridesmaids if they are willing to split some or all of the cost. Other guests should not be asked for financial contributions, although the bride's mother might volunteer to donate some cash. Just be sure, if you do accept such an offer, that she knows that the hosting duties and decision making still belong to you.

The Guest List

Bridesmaids, members of both families, and close friends may be invited. Customarily, the gathering is made up of just women, although mixed showers, often called "Jack-and-Jill showers," are increasingly common. The rule of thumb is that everyone invited to the shower should be invited to the wedding, although there are exceptions—for example, when the shower is thrown by coworkers, or when the couple is having a very small wedding at a faraway location. Some guests will be invited to one shower only, and others, especially the maid of honor and bridesmaids, may be invited to several.

Getting Started

Consult the bride about whom to invite. This way, the bride who will be given several showers can group her friends so that no one needs to attend too many showers or produce too many gifts. Alternatively, you may plan a surprise shower—they are traditional and can be great fun—but be aware of the bride's busy schedule. Also, be sensitive to the bride who doesn't like surprises. See Sassy Shower Themes (page 68) for entertaining ideas, and discuss the options in detail with the other bridesmaids. Especially when the other bridesmaids are helping to finance or host the event, be sure that they are all on board.

The Gift

Hosting the party does not get you off the gift-giving hook! Plan to spend somewhere between fifteen and fifty dollars. You can adorn your present with a fresh flower or other memorable trimming to add ambience to the gift table. If the bride prefers that guests donate money to a charity of her choice instead of bringing presents—this is not unheard of—arrange a pretty, beribboned collection basket for the donations, with extra envelopes placed nearby for guests who forgot to bring one.

For more ideas, see Gift Suggestions (page 60).

THE ENGAGEMENT PARTY

Unlike the bridal shower and bachelorette party, which are held months after the couple's engagement, this event is held promptly after the couple goes public with the happy news. The party happens before wedding plans are finalized, often before the bridesmaids are chosen, and there are no hard-and-fast rules about who should host (although traditionally the bride's parents get dibs on the first engagement celebration).
Any friend or relative may organize the occasion, so you can certainly volunteer—but if the bride chooses you to be her maid of honor or bridesmaid, you may also have to host a bridal shower and bachelorette party. Think through any offers before you make them. At this early stage, you don't want to spread your budget or bubbly hostess personality too thin.

The most traditional engagement party is an intimate event that serves as a first-time mixer for the couple's close friends and family members, but these days a casual celebration with a large guest list is also common. If you do host the event, consult the bride and groom about the guest list.

Giving a gift at an engagement party is not essential, although this depends on the style of the party: at a big cocktail affair, it's less likely that presents will be expected, while at an intimate party, gift giving would be more appropriate. When in doubt, ask the hostess when you RSVP where the couple is registered and whether you should bring a present. The gift doesn't have to be anything fancy—something small from the bridal registry will do the trick. One general rule of thumb is to spend approximately half of what you plan to spend on the shower gift.

Shower Invitations

Sending invitations creates a desirable ambience around the shower and helps any slightly frazzled hostess feel more organized (although for more casual showers, they are certainly not required). Try getting them out four weeks in advance, to give long-distance friends and relatives advance warning so they can get affordable airfares. If you are pressed for time or have a long guest list, you may choose preprinted invites to which you simply add the date, time, and other details. If you have a moment, however, handmade cards add a lovely, personal touch. Crafty types should consider making simple but elegant invites of sturdy card stock covered by sheer vellum, attached with colorful ribbon threaded through a couple of punched holes. Another thoughtful approach is to find some charming, quirky stationery—if the bride loves the ocean, for example, find cards with a shell or starfish print—and write the invitations in your own hand. You may word it as follows:

You are invited to attend a bridal shower

in honor of Sarah Putman

Sunday, May tenth, at five o'clock

3322 Santa Clara Street, San Francisco, California

RSVP to Emily Miller

(415) 555-8605

If you wish to include the name of the host in the first line, it would read, "Emily Miller invites you to attend a shower in honor of . . ."

If the event has a theme, such as a Linen Shower, you may insert that on the second line, above the date and time. If you have a deadline by which you need guests to respond, try writing, "Please RSVP to Emily Miller by May thirtieth." Ultimately, the wording of an invitation can be as specific or as general as the hostess deems appropriate—although including bridal registry information is an etiquette no-no. It's simply considered impolite to write the name of the stores

where the bride is registered on the invitation, or include her bridal registry card in the envelope. The safest way to disclose her registry information is the old-fashioned way, by word of mouth: ask the bridesmaids and the bride's family members for help spreading the news.

Remember to run the guest list by the bride one last time before putting the envelopes in the mail—and remember that, despite the work involved, a carefully chosen or created invitation will charm its recipients and set the stage for the bridal shower.

Party Favors

There are *real* favors—like accompanying a friend to her dull office party or giving her a ride to the airport at midnight—and then there are *bridal shower* favors. The latter do not involve a display of devotion or any personal sacrifice; they are simply small gifts given to guests at the shower. A hostess might bestow them on guests when they arrive or as they leave, or she may keep them in a basket to distribute during the party games, as prizes for winners.

At an elegant gathering, offerings might include small potted plants, miniature books of poetry, classy soaps and lotions, half bottles of champagne or Chardonnay, gourmet jams or scone mixes, packets of seeds, or gift cards and stationery. For a crowd of ladies who appreciate kitsch, Magic Eight Balls, body glitter, astrology scrolls, nail polish, and mood rings make a fun mix of gifts. If you plan to give favors as game prizes, be sure to have plenty on hand—for five group games, have around a dozen wrapped items. That way, if several people tie for first place, each can claim an award. If you will be simply giving the favors at the door, have enough for everyone, plus a few extras.

The last word: Unless crafting comes naturally to you, making complicated things like handmade fabric boxes as favors might be more trouble than it's worth. Save your time and energy for entertaining the guests! And keep in mind that, while a basket of colorful, prettily wrapped packages will certainly enhance the shower ambience, you shouldn't break your budget getting gifts for the guests. This party is more about the lovely bride than anyone else!

Gift Guidelines

The custom of "showering" brides with gifts began long ago, when brides went from house to house in the village to announce the engagement, and neighbors bestowed upon them some small gift from their household. Now, shower gifts are carefully chosen and decidedly elegant—and giving an old, used skillet would be considered hilariously uncouth!

At most bridal showers, the main event is watching the bride open her gifts. While this allows everyone a chance to see their gift opened with ceremony and be personally and graciously thanked by the bride or couple, it encourages guests to be competitive in their gift-giving. According to etiquette, however, giving lavish presents at bridal showers is not in good taste—and neither is the evolution of the simple shower into a consumer frenzy where friends feel pressured to prove their buying power. The most appropriate and classic shower gift is a practical and affordable household item. So spread the news and reverse the trend—and don't feel embarrassed if your gift seems simple in comparison to the others. In such cases, the guests bringing the very expensive gifts are being unmannerly by making the rest of the group feel self-conscious.

Most of all, remember that the real point of all the prewedding parties, fanfare, and gifts is to make the bride feel special and help her prepare for married life—not to prove how much you care about her by spending boatloads. Even flush bridesmaids can feel financially squeezed during the months leading up to a wedding, and knowing when to avoid a splurge can keep you sane through the nonstop gift giving and parties. As long as your offering is lovingly chosen and personally or prettily wrapped, it will be a welcome addition at the shower.

If you are invited to attend more than one shower, rules of etiquette suggest that purchasing one gift—and either sending it to the bride in the mail or offering it at any one of the showers—is preferable to bringing smaller, cheaper gifts to each of the parties. Any thoughtful bride will understand that you simply can't afford to bring equally elegant gifts to all of the showers. Similarly, graciously declining a second or third shower invitation is perfectly fine! You're better off missing the party if the idea of giving multiple gifts, or losing your one free afternoon, makes you feel even remotely bitter about being a bridesmaid. After all, attending showers is just one of your duties, and surviving the long haul to the wedding without feeling harried is more important than attending every little event along the way.

Fabulous Tip

HOW TO DEAL WITH BIG SPENDERS

Some bridesmaids are constantly brainstorming new ideas for group shower gifts for the bride, even after the group has decided on one or two specific items. When this spendy bridesmaid pressures everyone else to make endless additional contributions, major friction and financial distress can ensue in the ranks. Often, what makes this high-rolling girl so eager to empty her pockets (and yours) is guilt. Plagued with remorse about missing one of the bridal parties or an old friendship trauma—and hoping to redeem herself by giving presents—she pressures herself and everyone else into buying "just one more thing." When you are forced to deal with this big spender, politely explain that despite your never-ending love for the bride, you simply don't have any money left after buying the bridesmaid dress, arranging to attend the showers, and purchasing the gifts. As an alternative, you could offer to go in on the suggested gift as a wedding present.

Gift Suggestions

Many showers have themes that provide guidelines for gift giving. Traditional themes include linen showers and around-the-clock showers. If there is no theme, check the bridal registry for gift ideas, or let your imagination be your guide. Below are some specific suggestions.

Linen Shower

Any high-quality kitchen store should offer a lovely, colorful assortment of linen napkins and placemats for a reasonable price. Also, the gift doesn't literally have to be linen—for example, top-quality sheets with a high thread count or a set of plush towels would be welcome at this event.

Around-the-Clock Shower

At this theme shower, each guest is assigned a time of day and brings a gift that would be appropriate for that hour. Guests assigned the morning hours might bring coffee cups, a waffle maker, or a set of cozy flannel pajamas for weekend lounging. Gifts for the afternoon and evening might range from gardening tools to a bottle of fine wine. This party definitely allows guests room to be creative.

No Specified Theme

Check the bridal registry for something in your price range. Alternatively, consider some of the following ideas:

○ A gift certificate that fits her interests and needs—a framing store or home-accessories store are each a good bet

○ Theater tickets, or dinner for two at her favorite restaurant

○ Deruta-style serving bowls, plates, or pitchers

○ For the gardener, hand-selected seed packets, garden tools, and accessories

○ A cookbook and accessories chosen by theme—for example, a book on classic Spanish paella, paired with a pan and imported rice used in the traditional preparation of the dish

A Planning Checklist

Get on the ball early with this detailed to-do list.

Three Months Before the Shower
The truth is, although you can start planning three months in advance, you don't absolutely have to (call it honest procrastination). If you are eager to start planning, begin on the tasks listed below. Otherwise, just start mulling over some of the big things, like where you might hold the party and what style of entertaining your budget can accommodate.

Two Months Before the Shower
Consult the bride, and decide on the guest list together. (If you're hosting a surprise shower, consult the bride's mother or another family member.)

Get the addresses and telephone numbers of everyone on the guest list.

Decide on a shower theme so you can establish the type of food, drink, and atmosphere you want for the party.

Choose the location.

Get in touch with the key players: the bride's mother, sisters, and aunts; her oldest friend from grade school who was invited to the wedding but can't make it; and the bridesmaids, of course.

Coordinate schedules so everyone can attend.

Decide on favors.

One Month Before the Shower
Finalize the date and time.

Distribute invitations by mail or, for a very casual party, by telephone or e-mail.

Decide on games. They're the heart and soul of every fabulous shower.

Enlist help from the bridesmaids by giving them specific tasks. For example, "Betty, could you watch the wine on the buffet table during the party, and bring out new chilled bottles when necessary?"

Make or purchase favors.

Buy your gift.

The Week Before the Shower
Confirm RSVPs.

Confirm that the bridesmaids know their specific tasks.

Confirm food, flower, or cake orders, as well as delivery or pickup times.

Buy groceries and liquor or wine.

Decide on decorations, estimate how long it will take you to put them up, and purchase necessary items.

Assemble pens, pencils, Xeroxes, fruit, or other items necessary for shower games.

Assemble and gift-wrap favors.

Decide what you'll wear. Seriously. Don't wait until the last minute and discover you forgot to dry clean your cutest dress.

○ The Day Before the Shower
Prepare any food items that can be made in advance.

Talk to the bridesmaids to make sure they know their duties.

Run last-minute errands.

○ The Day of the Shower
Get to the party site early, with fresh flowers or other decorating supplies.

Finish preparing food, or receive or pick up food orders.

Set up decorations and seating.

Arrange flowers and food on tables.

Be fabulous!

Word Alert

❧ CANAPÉS ❧

If you know exactly what this word means, you probably own lots of cookbooks. If you don't know, here's a simple description: any type of delightful little snack served on tiny toast.

Usage: The bride's mother says to you, "Are you planning on making canapés for the bridal shower?"

Correct Response: "I'm still planning the menu."

(**Read:** I'm the hostess and I'll do what I please.)

THE BEST ICE-BREAKERS
(GAMES YOU WANT TO PLAY!)

Looking for the perfect game to bring shower guests together without boring them to tears? The multipurpose, multigenerational games that follow are the perfect solution! They're inexpensive to plan and easy to play, and they work equally well at a shower and at a bachelorette. One warning: Before you pick your game, imagine how it will strike your guests. If it focuses on the bride's childhood, newer acquaintances may feel left out. An overly libidinous game may offend the older folks. The best way to avoid ruffling feathers is to choose a funny, lively game that isn't too racy or revealing about the bride and her past.

Fabulous Bridal Quiz

Since this creative game puts the bride in the spotlight, everyone can be an expert and anyone can win! Whether the vibe at your party is slightly sexy, surprisingly quirky, or sweetly tame, you can tailor the questions on this quiz to fit your crowd. Guarantees a great time for groups of any size!

⊰ PREP WORK ⊱

Type up the quiz and make enough copies to distribute to all of your guests. (Easy to assemble at work!) Collect plenty of pencils and pens to hand out at the party.

THE BRIDE [insert name] **AND GROOM** [insert name] **TRIVIA CHALLENGE**
Please circle one answer only per question.

Sample questions and answers:

Where were the bride and groom when he proposed?

a ⊱ In Tuscany

b ⊱ Stuck in traffic

c ⊱ At home on the sofa

How long did the bride and groom know each other before they became engaged?

a ⊱ Since dinosaurs ruled the earth

b ⊱ Two years

c ⊱ Six months

What's the bride's biggest pet peeve about the groom?

a ⸙ His hobby of building beer-can pyramids while in his underwear

b ⸙ His refusal to wear underwear

c ⸙ His style of dress

Is the bride a natural blonde? (Circle one.)

Yes   No

Other sample questions:

What's the groom's middle name?

How did these two lovebirds meet?

What does the bride think is the groom's best feature?

Where did the groom grow up?

The questions and answers can be as earnest, playful, or naughty as you want—as long as your attitude is in step with the bride's. Creating a personalized quiz will not only make everyone laugh, it will also make the bride feel special. Asking questions that are open for interpretation—like whether or not she is a natural blonde, even if her bought-and-paid-for highlights are common knowledge—makes reading out the answers even more fun. (With this question in particular, the guests often split into camps, with the bride's loyal friends backing up her natural blonde status, and the older crowd laughing and taking the opposite position.) When crafting your quiz, be sure to consider the feelings of any older relatives or family friends who might be in attendance. Try to come up with ten to fifteen questions and answers.

⸙ **HOW TO PLAY** ⸙

Print out the quiz and make copies to distribute at the shower (try playful pink or floral-edged paper). Give everyone a few minutes to respond to the questions—but not so long that people start exchanging answers! If there is a tie, the bride can read off bonus questions that you've prepared especially for this scenario. Be sure the bonus round includes some zingers—everyone likes to see the bride blush. When a winner is selected, she (or he) gets to choose a gift from the basket of favors.

Plant the Kiss on Mr. Darcy

Lively enough to keep mischievous bridesmaids happy, yet chaste enough to be enjoyed by grandmothers and aunts, this funny and festive game is a crowd pleaser! If *Pride and Prejudice* isn't the bride's thing, substitute another favorite literary character or celebrity who lights her fire.

Locate photographs or drawings of the man in question. To find photographs of Colin Firth, who has played Mr. Darcy on the celebrated television miniseries, try doing a name search on the Internet. You may also have luck looking for feature articles in glossy magazines. Print or cut out the photographs, and make at least one hundred copies. (Don't worry if the quality is terrible! That really isn't the point.) If her dream stud's likeness is unavailable, trace a life-size figure on a roll of butcher paper, cut it out with scissors, and write his name at the top. Bring a tube of dark lipstick and a scarf or bandana to the party.

In a room of the apartment or house where the party will happen, tape the copied photographs of Mr. Darcy on the walls and doors. At least one wall should be completely papered over with his image. When you usher the bride-to-be inside, be prepared to bolster her with a drink—she might feel weak at the sight of so much masculine beauty!

{ HOW TO PLAY }

Any guest can go first. Have her apply a thick coat of lipstick, and then blindfold her with the scarf or bandana. As in Pin the Tail on the Donkey, turn her in a circle three times in one direction, and three times in the other. Then turn her so she's facing the wall papered over with the images of Mr. Darcy, and give her a gentle nudge in the right direction.

The object of the game is for her to kiss Mr. Darcy on the lips—the winner is the guest who leaves her mark closest to the correct area. Of course, you can also give a second prize for the kiss that lands in the most creative spot.

Two Truths and a Lie (a Bridal-Party Version)

This old favorite becomes excellent fun when given the right bridal-party spin, and it breaks the ice better than any game around. Plus, the guests do the creative work, so the hostess is off the hook.

PREP WORK

A few days before the party, ask each of the guests to brainstorm three statements about the bride—two should be true, and one should be false. The idea is to make it difficult for other guests to discern which is fact and which is fiction. For example:

"Susan played the tuba in high school."

"Susan once drank three shots of tequila and streaked across her college quad."

"Susan is marrying a man who wears his socks to bed."

Encourage guests to include funny and interesting tidbits from the bride's past. The more outrageous the true statements are, the harder it will be for guests to identify the lie. (This game works well on the spur of the moment, if you forget to prepare in advance.)

HOW TO PLAY

Have guests sit in a circle. Choose one guest to start things off by telling her two truths and a lie. She should try to keep a poker face—if she bursts out laughing when she says the lie, everyone will know the truth! After her statements have been made, the speaker, and the bride, keep quiet while the other guests speculate—"Would she really have done that?" The bride gets to listen to the debate, and hilarity always ensues. Everyone in the group then votes on a slip of paper for the statement they believe is the lie. (In small groups, you can vote by hand raising.) Finally, after the votes have been tallied and the results have been announced, the bride reveals the truth! If the speaker lied convincingly enough to get everyone to vote for her lie, she wins a gift from the basket of favors. Move on to the next guest until everyone has had her turn.

Fabulous Tip

THE GAME TO STAY AWAY FROM

The traditional Clothespin Game in which every guest wears a clothespin until they screw up by saying the forbidden word— usually "wedding"—remains popular despite being rather tedious. The truth is, any fabulous bridesmaid will say the forbidden word right off, just to get that pesky clothespin off her outfit. Skip this game in favor of something more daring to turn any ho-hum bridal shower into a hilarious party.

Sassy Shower Themes

When the bride and the ambience surrounding her wedding are more quirky than traditional, try one of these sassy themes on for size. Each description below offers the total package—hot tips for the hostess, fabulous entertaining ideas, and excellent games to break the ice—everything you need to turn a simple shower into a superlative celebration. Whether you take a traditional route or host something entirely offbeat, a bridal shower should reflect the bride's tastes and personality. In addition to considering what she might like, think about your budget, the size of the guest list, the possible venues, and the type of crowd you'll be catering to. Also, consider your own strengths, and be sure to recruit lots of help. Any obstacle can be overcome with a crack team of bridesmaids to help you.

Wear your Whites: An Outdoor Extravaganza

For the sporting bride-to-be, what could be more fun than an afternoon of croquet or badminton—especially when the real point is to drink mint juleps and wear crisp whites? This shower is great for large groups. While an outdoor location is necessary, athletic skills are optional!

O **Hostess Hotline:** Finding a fun location is the first step. Any grassy backyard or pleasant park will do. (If you run into problems, persevere and do some research—perhaps the bride's aunt has a lovely home that would be the perfect venue.) Plan an on-the-go menu of cool drinks and elegant picnic fare. On the day of the party, arrive early to set up the croquet or badminton set, and learn the rules if you don't already know them. Once guests arrive, ply them with food and cocktails while clearly explaining how to play. Let the games begin, and you've got a party.

O **Gifts:** Anything white. Gifts can be as practical as crisp white sheets, white table linens, or white kitchen appliances, or more conceptual, like a framed black-and-white photograph or a fabulous bottle of white wine. Encourage guests to be creative!

○ **Game:** Play a theme-party version of *The Newlywed Game*. In advance, ask the groom questions that involve the color white: For a vacation, would he rather go white-water rafting or snowboard on fresh powder? Which item of white clothing does he wear most often: white BVDs, white socks, or tight white jeans? Would he rather listen to Whitesnake (hard rock), Average White Band (disco), or Barry White (soul)? The bride—and all the guests—have to pick which answers they think the groom would choose. The more ridiculous the questions, the better. (If you don't have time to get his answers in advance, use the bride's answers as the key.) The guest who guesses the most answers correctly wins a prize.

SHOWER THEME ALTERNATIVES

If you prefer not to follow a theme, try simple entertaining options such as an evening of desserts and coffee or a casual mid-morning brunch. (With a no-theme shower, guests can bring gifts of their own choosing, although you might circulate, by word of mouth, the names of the stores where she's registered.) Or you can patch together your own unique party by adapting a traditional theme to meet your needs.

For example, if the bride wants to grill steaks and play sports at the shower but needs classy table linens for her home, you can hold a barbecue in the park with beer and Frisbee games—and use the Linen Shower gift theme. There's no rule saying that the entertainment at bridal showers has to be prim and proper!

Wine Tasting: A Spirited Celebration

An indoor or outdoor bar setup will add to the ambience. Even something as simple as a long table covered with a crisp white cloth will do the trick—display the wineglasses and vintages you will be pouring. This theme works equally well at a ladies-only or mixed shower.

○ **Hostess Hotline:** Try serving your guests a "flight," three to six different types of the same varietal. A Merlot or Cabernet Sauvignon works well as the varietal of choice because there are so many excellent and affordable vintages available in stores. If you have a specialty wine store nearby, you could consult the experts there and try a flight of something more esoteric, such as French Côtes du Rhône, or Italian Barbera. Flights can work equally well for drinks other than wine, such as sake or tequila.

Alternatively, you could do a more traditional wine tasting, with a progression from whites to reds, as follows: Sauvignon Blanc, Chardonnay, Pinot Noir, Merlot, Cabernet Sauvignon. Be sure to ask the person pouring to remember that only a taste should be poured into each glass, just enough to swirl the liquid and have one or two sips.

○ **Gifts:** The easiest gift is a bottle of fine wine for the bride's cellar, although glasses, corkscrews, wine racks, and subscriptions to food or wine magazines would also fit the bill.

○ **Game:** With a particularly wine-savvy crowd, play this version of the name game: Write out the names of different wines on index cards (for example, California Chardonnay, French Bordeaux, Australian Shiraz, Italian Chianti), and pin a card to every guest's back. Guests must query the people around them to help them figure out what sort of wine they are. The silly questions you have to ask make this game fun: "Am I red or white?" "Am I full bodied?" "Am I French, Italian, or American?" All the reds have to find each other, and the same goes for whites. When everyone has guessed their wine type and found their group, the wine tasting can begin.

Note: This theme can work wonderfully at a Jack-and-Jill shower. For a casual event, you might consider having each guest or couple attending the shower bring two bottles of wine—one for the party and one for the bride and groom's cellar.

Culinary Queen: A Girls' Dinner Gala

This dinner party bridal shower has a wonderful, intimate feel. It works best when the guest list is small, so everyone can sit down together to enjoy the meal—and enjoy watching the bride eat with gusto!

○ **Hostess Hotline:** Organize a dinner party, and drive the bride wild with delicacies! Whether her favorite food is the native cuisine of France, Italy, or India—or anywhere in between—you can create a fabulous four-course menu by cribbing from a classic cookbook. For French cooking, anything by Julia Child will do, and for Italian food, search out books by Marcella Hazan. For Indian food, try any of Madhur Jaffrey's cookbooks. Add to the ambience by playing music that fits your culinary theme—whether it's French pop, Italian opera, or Indian sitar ragas—and go all out with festive table linens, candles, and elegant serving dishes. Throw the bride's favorite cocktail or wine into the mix, and this dinner can be one of the most memorable meals of her life! (This much cooking takes teamwork, so get all of the bridesmaids on board in advance, get organized, and have a fun day together in the kitchen.)

○ **Gifts:** Specialty cookware, cookbooks, gourmet foods, and other kitchen-related items.

○ **Game:** Wrap a variety of spices—preferably those used in the dishes you're serving—in small aluminum packets with holes poked in them. Pass the packets around the circle so guests can sniff them and try to name each spice correctly. It's surprisingly hard! The one who has identified the most spices correctly at the end of the round wins a prize.

Fabulous Tip

HOW TO MAKE THE LOPSIDED CAKE YOU BAKED FOR THE BRIDAL SHOWER LOOK GOOD

Lop off the uneven tops with a dental-floss guillotine, and pad layers generously with thick, rich frosting.

Bridal Tea: An Afternoon of Elegance

When the guest list includes ladies ages eight to eighty, a traditional tea party is an excellent way to entertain. Leave complicated shower themes and rowdy party games behind, and have a simple afternoon of charming conversation, delicious finger sandwiches, and strong tea served in delicate china cups.

○ **Hostess Hotline:** A pleasant, summery garden full of golden afternoon light is the ideal setting for this classic bridal event. Rent or borrow enough folding chairs or garden furniture so that the majority of folks can sit down, and consider making a special seat for the bride festooned with streamers, flowers, or white tulle, so she can sit in high style while opening her gifts. The buffet table should be a party highlight, with fresh flowers and a delicious array of treats. Lay out silver trays of finger sandwiches and plates of delicate lemon shortbread, fresh strawberries, currant scones, and clotted cream. Have tea cozies on hand to keep the teapots warm, and serve the tea with cream and sugar, or lemon, in delicate teacups with saucers. You may also serve a light cocktail, such as mimosas, or a chilled, crisp white wine.

○ **Gifts:** Rather than specifying any gift theme on the invitation, let the guests bring what they please—the traditional style of the party will inspire most guests to bring a traditional gift, either an item from the bridal registry or simply a classic gift for the couple's home. Spread the information about where the bride is registered by word of mouth (including "registry cards" with the invitation is considered tacky). If guests ask you for further guidance, tell them that any traditional item for the kitchen, bedroom, or bath would be welcomed.

○ **Games:** This classic tea party calls for the tried-and-true games that have become bridal shower standards. Here are a few of the most amusing time-honored favorites.

Ribbon Bouquet

This old tradition will charm the older folks in the crowd, although it's more of a one-person activity than a game. Using the ribbons from the shower gifts, a bridesmaid creates a mock bouquet by threading the ribbons through a hole in a paper-plate base. According to tradition, the ribbons represent the bride's fertility—the more ribbons, the more children she will have. (With the number of gifts at showers these days, let's hope nobody actually ends up with a kid for every ribbon!) The bride can carry the mock bouquet at the wedding rehearsal and do the traditional toss, or simply keep it as a piece of memorabilia.

Wedding Night Preview

While the bride opens her gifts, a bridesmaid secretly writes down the bride's exclamations. For example, "I know just where to put these!" or "Can you show me how this works?" When all of the gifts have been opened, the mischievous maid will come forward and read the bride's comments aloud, describing them as the words of passion she will spout on her wedding night.

Toilet Paper Bride

Divide the shower guests into groups of six or fewer, and put the groups in different rooms. Give each group several rolls of toilet paper, several white garbage bags, and a few paper clips. One person from each group is the model—mothers or mothers-in-law-to-be make excellent ones—and other team members dress her in a bridal gown, fashioning it from the materials they've been given (no tape or scissors allowed). The bride gets to wander around and watch the festivities, judge the final fashion show, and pick the winner.

EASY FINGER SANDWICHES

INGREDIENTS

Plain white bread
Cream cheese
Peeled cucumber, or watercress leaves

Find a good, plain white bread—not too dense, but not full of air, either—
preferably thinly sliced. Avoid strong-flavored breads, like sourdough
or those flavored with herbs or cheese. Stack up several slices at once,
cutting off the crusts with a serrated knife. Spread a thin layer of cream
cheese (do not use the reduced-fat type) on each slice of bread. To make
the sandwiches, layer thin slices of peeled cucumber, or watercress leaves,
between the prepared slices of bread. Cut each sandwich into quarters.
Repeat until you have 48 finger sandwiches, and arrange on a silver tray.
Serves 12.

Couples Barbecue Bash: A Jack-and-Jill Shower

Perfect for the easygoing bride who loves big, zany parties, this theme shower is
great for including the guys. A large backyard or park lawn is ideal, so you can
barbecue safely and have plenty of space to spread out during the games.

○ **Hostess Hotline:** Jack-and-Jill showers are most successful when they include
themes that interest both the bride and groom. While many still feature the
traditional gift-opening event, the main activities should be eating, drinking,
and games—and when the guest list is large, you may dispense with opening
the gifts altogether. (It can be hard to have fun if the entire afternoon is spent
watching the couple open presents; besides, the bride and groom may feel
relieved to get out of performing for such a large audience.) When it comes to
hostessing, the duties here are light! All you have to do is get some juicy steaks
or burgers to throw on the grill, pick up a selection of salads and condiments at
your local deli, and order a keg (or two) of cold beer—and if you can convince

one of those barbecue-loving guys to take over your cooking duties, you can sit back and enjoy!

Although mixed showers are increasingly popular, some etiquette experts view them as tacky, since inviting so many guests can seem like a brazen bid for more booty. The prevailing view, however, is that such events can be an excellent way for the bride's and groom's families, as well as friends of both sexes, to get acquainted before the wedding. Still, with this in mind, be sure that the bride, and her mother, are on board for inviting the guys before you start the planning process.

O **Gifts:** Barbecue-related items such as tongs, serving dishes, aprons, or cookbooks will work well; you can also expand the gift theme to include backyard items, from hammocks or casual lawn chairs to garden tools and plants. If the guest list is particularly large, however, you may want to omit gift suggestions and let people bring items from the registry, or whatever they think the couple will enjoy, to ensure that the bride and groom don't receive more outdoor accessories than would be useful.

O **Games:** Great fun can be had when you split the crowd into teams and pit the men against the women in a good-natured battle of the sexes. You can even kick off the competition by having the two teams compete to create the best burger combination, to be judged by the father of the bride. Here are a couple more inspirational ideas:

Quiz Show

Make up two Fabulous Bridal Quizzes (see pages 64–65), one for the bride and one for the groom. On the bride's quiz, ask questions about the groom, or about men in general; on the groom's quiz, ask questions about the bride, or women in general. Then divide the guests into male and female teams. The women try to guess how the groom responded to the questions, and the men try to guess the bride's answers. When the teams are finished, the bride and groom—who have completed their respective quizzes separately, before the party began—reveal their answers.

Relay Madness

In this hilarious relay race, each team member must put on flippers, run across a lawn, and try to flip a plastic goldfish into a butterfly net held by one of their team members. It sounds strange, but it's fun! Have the teams line up side-by-side, with one member from each team standing across the lawn holding the butterfly net, and on the count of three, begin the relay. If you don't have enough space to play outdoors, you could have both teams compete to see who can build the larger structure out of playing cards.

BRIDAL SHOWER SCRAPBOOK

No matter what type of bridal shower you host, making a scrapbook to commemorate the occasion is the cherry on the sundae, the frosting on the cake—the extra-special touch that makes the event even more memorable for the bride.

Consult with the bridesmaid team and decide as a group what kind of scrapbook you want to create, or make an executive decision if the project is on your shoulders. (Keep in mind that having the bridesmaids contribute will help you manage the expenses of buying Polaroid film or developing the photographs.) A puffy, glittery book from a kid's novelty shop filled with hilarious Polaroids from the party will make a kitschy treasure, while a book crafted of beautiful, handmade paper filled with stylish black-and-white shots will have a more elegant feel. When deciding on the approach, take cues from your budget—

those handmade paper books can run upwards of one hundred bucks—and the bride's preferences.

The most essential part of the scrapbook, however, is personalizing it by writing all sorts of sassy notes in the margins! You can rely on the bridesmaids to provide editorial input after the party is over, or attempt to get the bride's friends and family to contribute to the scrapbook while the bridal shower is under way. If you wish to try the latter, appoint a bridesmaid to spirit guests away from the party at discreet moments, bringing them to a quiet room where they can write in the scrapbook unseen by the bride. (One benefit of Polaroids is that you can pen notes in the white margins of the pictures themselves!) Have a selection of colorful, glittery pens available, so the commentary itself adds a design element to the scrapbook.

If you want to use traditionally developed photographs instead of Polaroids, appoint a bridal shower shutterbug: her photographic skill isn't as important as her willingness to put aside her drink and focus on capturing the best, funniest, and most memorable moments of the shower. (Hint: Don't try to play photographer if your hands will be busy with hosting duties.)

The scrapbook can also include the shower invitation, lovely bits of ribbon or wrapping paper, mementos of the games you played, and the label from a particularly nice vintage of champagne you served—in short, whatever objects you like to complete the picture of the bridal shower.

If you're ambitious and good with follow-through, start the scrapbook
at the bridal shower, but expand the idea to create a visual journal of her
entire tour as a bride. Choose a durable, leather-bound book that will last forever, and include mementos from the bridal shower, the bachelorette party,
the rehearsal dinner, and the wedding; invitations, photographs, copies of
toasts and speeches, and notes from the bride's dearest friends and family
members are welcome additions. Since creating such a scrapbook takes considerable time, money, and effort, you may consider giving it as the wedding
gift—after all, memories are the best present of all. She'll be touched by your
thoughtfulness every time she pulls the book from a drawer.

THE BACHELORETTE PARTY

When their bride-love and budget have been challenged
by the dress buying, bridal shower hosting, and constant
emotional counseling—and the big day is still a month
away—some bridesmaids have been known to wonder
whether the bachelorette party is really necessary. In
fact, few things are more essential!

THE BIG PICTURE

No polite gift-opening gabfest can replace the bachelorette bash, for the
bride or the bridesmaids, since this is the only prewedding party where everyone can let her hair down, fling aside worries over manners and etiquette, and
celebrate in her preferred style. This party is the bride's singleton swan song,
her rock-bottom last chance to celebrate the end of an era—and every bride
deserves one. In addition to providing a golden opportunity to bond with her
girls and blow off steam, the festivities will distract her from her bridal jitters
and wedding worries. This overview of bachelorette-party protocol puts
crucial information at your fingertips, so you can plan without stepping on
anyone's toes.

Hosting Duties

The bridesmaid troupe runs the show, with the maid of honor at the helm. This party is all about group effort, and everyone is a key player in making the night a blast. Each person involved should feel comfortable with the plan—if one of the maids is shy and balks at the idea of a boisterous night on the town, talk to her and change the itinerary if necessary.

Money Matters

Generally, the costs are split evenly among the bridesmaids or all of the guests—for example, close friends of the bride who are not in the wedding will usually chip in. Appoint the maid of honor or a bridesmaid to organize the finances and project costs, so everyone contributes equally and guests know the contribution amount in advance. You may want to include the cost of a group gift in the budget. The maid of honor may instead finance the party on her own, asking guests to bring a potluck dish or contribute only to the group gift.

The Guest List

Depending on the bride's wishes, invitations may be restricted to the bridal party, or, as is more often the case, they may be extended to some of the bride's other close friends or coworkers. The groom's sister and other important female wedding guests—for example, the best man's significant other—should be invited.

Getting Started

The bachelorette party shouldn't require quite as much formal planning as the bridal shower, although for basic guidelines you might follow those in A Planning Checklist (see page 62). Consult with all the bridesmaids on the entertainment options, especially if they are helping to foot the bill. Definitely discuss the guest list with the bride—there may be people outside her close circle of friends she feels compelled to invite. Generally, sending formal invitations isn't necessary—asking people via group e-mail or telephone is fine for this casual occasion—although sending silly invitations can set a humorous, fun tone for the festivities, and it may be the practical option for very large groups. Whatever route you choose, start early on nailing down the date—coordinating the schedules of a bunch of girls-on-the-go can take weeks!

Fabulous Tip

How to Make a Spectacle of the Bride (and Why She Deserves It)

One of the most hilarious diversions during the bachelorette festivities is to find little ways to embarrass the bride and generally make an enormous production over her in public. She asked to be in the spotlight by deciding to go through with this matrimonial madness—so let her have it! Perennial favorite ways to abash the bride include dressing her up in a cheesy bridal veil, cheap feather boa, or sparkly tiara, then taking her out on the town. For the rehearsal dinner, one option is to rewrite the lyrics to a popular song (try the slippery theme song of the movie *Titanic*) and gather the bridesmaids to sing it to her at the dinner, in front of her family and friends. Above all, the teasing should be good-natured, designed to appeal to the bride's sense of humor.

Smart Ways to Save at the Bachelorette Party

- Have a few rowdy rounds of cocktails and games at home before you hit the bar circuit.

- Prepare the hors d'oeuvres yourself, or with the other bridesmaids, instead of hiring caterers.

- If your party hits the town, choose a lively neighborhood with plenty of hot spots, so you can barhop on foot instead of spending a fortune on taxis.

- If you're having a house party, keep the food and decorations simple, and save your money for fun gifts and fabulous booze.

- Get creative with your games and decorations and make them yourself—no need to buy them unless you're really pressed for time.

- Whatever embarrassing garment you're going to make the bride wear in public—a bonnet, a feather boa, or a tiara, for example—find it in advance.

Make the Bride a Special Cocktail

Whether you're hosting an all-night house party for the bachelorettes, or mixing some cocktails for the ladies before the barhopping begins, few things will commemorate the occasion better than creating a brand-new cocktail in honor of the bride—and naming it after her!

Call it Sarah's Citrus Surprise or Anne's Champagne Aperitif, and she will be immortalized for the night—maybe for a lifetime, if you hit on the right concoction! Not sure how to begin? Pick her favorite poison, add her favorite mixers, then shake or stir with ice.

Gift Guidelines

The bachelorette party inspires funny and fabulous gifts—and not just the kind that cost money, either. While the group will probably want to chip in to get the bride something nice, crafting something creative in addition will go a long way toward making the evening special. Brainstorm with the bridesmaids to decide on the memento that will best capture the moment. The following ideas include some items that can be found in stores, and others that are meaningful, nostalgic gifts that only best friends can give. When the whole group shares the burden of effort and expense, it is easy to offer her both types of presents—the material *and* the more sentimental—while keeping costs at a minimum.

Classic Bachelorette Gifts

A blue garter that the bride can wear at her wedding is one traditional offering (it can function as the blue element of the "something old, new, borrowed, and blue" good-luck charm). Lingerie of any type is also a classic gift, especially gorgeous, expensive, slinky items that a practical bride might not purchase for herself. Fortunately, you don't have to go for broke, since everyone attending the party can and should contribute to the gift. Pick the price range, assign two bridesmaids to do the shopping, and have everyone chip in afterward.

Gift certificates are also a good bet because of their flexibility—you can give her a lavish spa treatment, or a fabulous massage. Another option is a certificate for a meal for two at her favorite restaurant. Theater tickets—or, if you want to splurge, a romantic bed-and-breakfast getaway—are also extremely thoughtful gifts. The wedding couple will probably be strapped for cash when they return from their honeymoon, and this way, romantic dinners and weekend getaways won't be out of the question.

Snapshot Time Line

Have every bridesmaid go through the old photographs she has of the bride and herself and pick out those that have special significance. Ask the ladies to show up at the party early and collaborate to make a time line on butcher paper. Tape the photographs in chronological order and write captions beneath each describing that moment in the bride's life. The chronology can include typical "big moments," like birthdays or graduations, or it can be more tongue-in-cheek. If you have a photograph of her from junior high with bad hair, for example, pin up the image with a caption that describes this moment as her **worst** bad-hair day. The quirkier your photos and captions, the funnier the time line will be. You can also include photographs that commemorate when she met each of the bridesmaids.

Farah Fawcett
meets Chewbacca

Depending on how long her bridesmaids have known her, the time line can begin at infancy, or start later, perhaps during her college years. Whether the time line is sentimental or sassy, this gift is something she can fold up and treasure forever.

Friendship Book

Get a nice blank journal and have every guest decorate a page or two, with anything from photographs and ticket stubs to poems and recipes, and dust the pages with glitter or adorn them with gold stars. Each of the entries will be unique and represent the particular kind of friendship that person shares with the bride. Somewhere on the page, each guest must include some piece of advice for the bride as she starts her new life. Ask the groom to contribute a page as well—he's likely to write incredibly sweet and earnest things. On the front of the book, create a colorful collage of favorite photographs of the bride and the friends who attend the bachelorette party. This gift is guaranteed to be moving as the bride pages through the book and sees how much she is loved.

BRIDESMAIDS' LUNCHEON

The first incarnation of the bachelorette party was the bridesmaids' luncheon, an all-girl event where the maids offered their group gift to the bride. Some bridesmaid troupes today still prefer this classy approach and may opt to host a luncheon instead of (or in addition to) a bachelorette party. More commonly these days, however, the bridesmaids' luncheon is hosted by the mother of the bride, as a way of thanking the bridesmaids for their hard work, and often bridesmaids will receive their gifts from the bride at this event.

If your bridal party does wish to host an elegant luncheon instead of an evening party, you may also want to give the bride the customary gift that went along with this tradition: a sterling silver tray, engraved with the initials of the bridesmaids.

UNFORGETTABLE BACHELORETTE BASHES

What makes bachelorette parties so fabulous isn't necessarily the drinking, games, or dancing, it's the fun of sashaying down the bride's memory lane! The more you celebrate the bride's unique style (and colorful past), the more memorable the evening will be. Whether you spend an evening at home with a fortune-teller, have a night of drinks and dancing on the town, or go all out for a deluxe weekend in Vegas, adding that personal touch—such as renting her favorite old movies to watch or playing the grooving dance tunes that you know make her booty move—will turn any basic bachelorette bash into party perfection. In other words, don't simply rely on the trappings of the occasion to make her feel special; find a creative way to relate the party particularly to her. Whether you choose to stay home, hit the highway, or take a tour of some hot local bars, the creative party themes that follow should get your idea engines revved up.

On The Town

A bachelorette party on the town makes the same impression on a run-of-the-mill bar as would an asteroid hitting earth—there's a just-burned-through-the-atmosphere force field around these girls, and they always leave a memorable impression! The point of taking your bachelorette party to the streets isn't simply to party, it's to create a spectacle, preferably one that involves feather boas, sparkly tiaras, and other fun accessories that might do the necessary job of embarrassing the bride. Whether you stick to the classic night-out routine or throw a curve ball by suggesting some of these creative ideas, hitting the town with the ladies rocks!

Fearless Ladies Party

The bride will be amazed when you let her out of the car at a trapeze studio! Most major cities have training studios for circus performers, and their classes offer a great opportunity for all-girl bonding. Indoor rock climbing is another excellent option, and climbing gyms have guides to show you the ropes (ask if they offer discounts for large beginner groups). Kickboxing can fit the bill if your guests prefer to keep their feet on the ground. Once the endorphin rush kicks in, you will be celebrating in style! Reward all that hard work with an indulgent night of fabulous cocktails and a sumptuous dinner.

If the bride's tastes run toward things retro, plan a slightly less extreme but still sporty roller-skating party. (The rinks still exist; it just takes some research and possibly a short road trip to get there.) To make the party more personal, find out which idol the bride loved as a teenybopper—in every girlhood lurks the secret of a slightly embarrassing crush. Whether her heart throbbed over Boyz II Men or Menudo, ask the roller-skating rink's disc jockey to play their songs and dedicate them to the bride.

Jenny's Ten Stop

This party fits the bill when the bride has tons of friends, wants all of them to celebrate with her, and has serious party stamina: the Ten Stop involves hitting ten bars in ten hours. The most convenient running time is from 4 P.M. to 2 A.M. Invitations should have a clearly marked map on the back so that guests who can't stay the whole time can pop in at that hour's bar for a quick drink or disco dance and offer congratulations to the bride-to-be. This party is an excellent option when you're having trouble finding a time that works for everyone, since nearly all the guests will be able to squeeze in at least a short visit at some point during the night. Include one or two fun restaurants on the itinerary, so guests aren't drinking for hours on empty stomachs, and a couple of dance spots where everyone can boogie down. (Of course, remember to swap in the name of the bride before the words "Ten Stop" on the invitation, or everyone will wonder who Jenny is, and why she didn't come.)

Royal Treatment Spa Day

Girl-bonding in the mud baths, sassy bachelorette giggles in the steam room, and fabulous manicures all around . . . hitting the spa with the ladies makes for one fabulous party! From volcanic mud treatments and mineral hot tubs to luxurious facials and Shiatsu massages, every spa offers something different. Do your research and make reservations according to what the bride and company prefer, but decide on a budget before you book the appointments— luxury spa treatments don't come cheap. Particularly if everyone in the group wants to chip in and get the bride something special in addition to paying for their own massages and facials, the individual donations will be considerable. In many cities, international neighborhoods offer options like Japanese baths, which are often less expensive than swanky downtown spas. Inquire about group activities when you're calling around. Many places are willing to seat friends together for mud baths or manicures so you can chat while receiving luxury treatments. An excellent way to celebrate and relax with the ladies, this afternoon of indulgence and intimacy will help the most stressed-out bride shore up her sanity.

Fabulous Tip

HOW TO MAKE SURE THE BRIDE GETS SPECIAL TREATMENT FROM THE BARTENDER

Ask the bartender to whip up a special drink you've concocted in advance (see Make the Bride a Special Cocktail, page 81). When he calls out her cocktail—for example, "Sarah's Citrus Surprise"—he'll be on a first-name basis with her!

Out of Town

When a one-night bachelorette party doesn't seem like enough celebration, it's time to start planning an all-out, all-weekend bachelorette extravaganza! Such occasions can present a slight financial challenge, since an extended party will require more than just petty cash, but if you have a tight-knit group of friends who are all willing to contribute, this event will be absolutely unforgettable.

Sin in the City

Nothing spells d-e-b-a-u-c-h-e-r-y better than a bachelorette party in a glitzy metropolitan area—so whether your bride prefers Manhattan or Miami, L.A. or Las Vegas, this urban getaway is all about glamour. You can have fun getting there, too—just don't party so hard on the plane that you're hungover when you arrive. When you go out, have your crew wear something fun, like specially designed matching baby tees or bright feather boas—costumes might seem silly at home, but in foreign territory, they are the spice of life! You can book hotels and flights for reasonable rates if you reserve in advance, but this hot party option will never be cheap, so make sure all the bridesmaids are cool with the idea before going ahead.

Time Capsule Weekend

Visit the bride's old stomping grounds! Create an itinerary designed to help her remember her roots. For example, you might start at the dive hot-dog stand near her college campus (the bride's favorite spot for late-night binge fests), move to the bar where she waitressed her senior year, then stop by somewhere she frequented, like the school football stadium or the dusty old library, and sneak inside to toss back a beer. After that, take it up a notch by taking a limo to that fancy bar where she went on her first date with her groom (if she knew him in college). Of course, include a side trip to that dive bar or dance club where she once kissed a stranger (or a few), just to remind her of her sketchy past. End the day with a slumber party on the floor of an apartment or hotel suite. The next morning, take a long walk before stopping at her favorite scenic spot for a casual brunch with mimosas and bagels, where everyone can make meaningful toasts about the next chapter in her life. The experience will be unforgettable, and the detailed itinerary itself—which will include the reason you're stopping at each place—will make an excellent keepsake for the bride.

HOW TO FEND OFF UNACCEPTABLE GUYS TRYING TO DIRTY DANCE WITH YOUR BACHELORETTE PARTY GUESTS

Form a tight dancing circle, using shoulders and elbows to box the guy out of your orbit. If he wants to know why you won't let him in, say something slightly denigrating about his appearance, such as, "Are you wearing a shirt under that vest?" When he looks confused and says "No," you can respond, "There you go." He'll be stunned and will slink back to wherever he came from.

House Parties

House parties are the best way to be fabulous on a budget, since you control the expenses—and you can decide in advance where to splurge and where to save. Plus, your bridal party can bond better without the interruptions of bar crowds and noise. Give into the temptation to stay at home with the girls! When you host one of the following parties, the bride will be blown away by your creativity and class, and your bank account won't go bust.

Storybook Soiree

Is there a dog-eared novel on her shelf that she reads over and over again? A movie she never gets tired of seeing? Let the story be the premise for your party: dress the bride like her favorite heroine, serve the appropriate foods, and design the decorations and games around the plot. Inspired by Jane Austen's book *Pride and Prejudice* (and the film version starring Colin Firth), this sample party will make any bride who loves the Bennett family absolutely ecstatic. If the nineteenth century isn't her thing, try *Breakfast at Tiffany's*.

Pride and Prejudice Party

○ Make her wear a bonnet.

○ Serve a buffet replete with nineteenth-century favorites like roast mutton.

○ Come up with the top ten ways the groom is like Mr. Darcy.

○ Play Plant the Kiss on Mr. Darcy (see page 66).

○ If you feel like embarrassing her further, take her out for drinks and make her ask the bartender if "a Mr. Darcy" has called for her—the look the bartender gives her before he shakes his head will be priceless.

○ Rent or buy the A&E series *Pride and Prejudice* and play it in the background.

Healing Waters Relaxation Party

With an aromatic foot soak and soothing herbal tea, this party brings the wedding troupe together for a night of domestic fun—all it takes is creating a "spa studio" in your home. Choose a room with lots of comfortable seating—provide armchairs, sofas, or futons, and enough pillows on the floor for everyone to get comfortable—and set the thermostat to at least seventy degrees. It should be warm enough for guests to wear cotton T-shirts without extra layers. Unplug the phone. On the stereo, play a soundtrack of waves and ocean sounds at low volume. Burn candles or sandalwood incense, and dim the lights. Handwrite a *Spa Studio* sign for the door of the room, so guests can have the experience of entering a separate, specifically calming place; on the sign, include a reminder to turn off cell phones. Ask your guests to bring or wear loose, comfortable clothing, so they can roll up their pants to soak their feet and feel completely unrestricted and relaxed.

As hostess, try to stay calm yourself, and communicate a vibe of well-being (pretty easy when you're sporting your favorite comfy clothes and flip-flops).

You might be a little busy when the guests first arrive, supplying hot water for the foot basins and brewing tea, but once everyone is soaking their feet in the warm, aromatic waters and sipping your healing herbal concoction, relaxation will wash over the group and the prep work will be 100 percent worth it. *Ahhhhhh.*

Healing Tea

Visit a natural food store or an herb shop and create a relaxing custom mix of whole tea leaves for the bride. Think about what healing she might need at that particular moment in time. Chamomile promotes relaxation, while peppermint invigorates. Ginseng energizes the mind and body, while calendula has a healing effect. Combine several different herbs to maximize taste and effect. For inspiration, research the blend of the bride's favorite store-bought herbal tea, or seek out someone at the store's herb counter for further advice.

In several glass Mason jars, mix the dried whole leaves together. Using ovals (or wedding bells) cut from construction paper, create handmade labels for the jars. Write in the name of the tea blend—Samantha's Stress Soother or Lisa's Lavender Twilight, for example, inspired by the bride in question—and put the jars out on a central table as decorative additions, or make enough to be given as party favors for guests.

A French press provides an excellent means of brewing a healing herbal tea blend made from whole leaves. (The average French press will generally make four cups of tea. For a large guest list, have several on hand—you can buy or borrow. If you're buying, look for the plastic type, which are generally cheaper and should be easy to find at a kitchen store. Call first to make sure they carry them.) While the loose herbs steep in the water, they give off a lovely, soothing aroma, so set the French presses on the table in the "spa studio." Serve the tea with honey and wedges of lemon in Japanese-style ceramic teacups.

Aromatic Soak

Purchase a plastic basin for each guest, making sure each is large enough to comfortably accommodate both feet at once. From a body lotion shop or natural food store, purchase some essential oil—try tangerine or eucalyptus for an invigorating soak, or lavender or sandalwood for a soothing experience.

When all the guests have arrived, they should seat themselves comfortably and take off their shoes and socks while the hostess, and a helper or two, fill the individual basins with hot water from the tub or sink. The water temperature shouldn't be scalding, but it should be quite warm—enough to compensate for how quickly the hot water will cool in the air. Add a few drops of the aromatic oil to the filled basin and swirl it around so the scent is appreciable. Bring the basins and a towel to each guest. The hostess should fill her own basin last, make sure everyone has a cup of tea, and then slip her own feet into the warm, healing waters.

The aromatic foot soak will make everyone feel pampered and will contribute to whole-body relaxation, but you can take it one step further with a group do-it-yourself pedicure session. (You can even ask each guest to contribute a polish in their favorite fun color.) Have the following supplies in your spa studio:

- Cheap pairs of flip-flops or toe separators for every guest, for smudge-free nail-polish drying

- Tools for nail finishing, such as files and buffers

- Rich, scented massage oil or invigorating peppermint foot lotion

- Nail-polish remover, cotton pads, and cotton swabs

- Top-notch nail polishes in a variety of colors, and clear gloss for base and top coats

Hibernation Rituals

Plenty of entertainers do house calls—and hiring talent can be affordable when the total cost is shared among the guests! Consult with the bridesmaids before procuring a professional, however, since this plan takes some commitment in advance. Changing the date at the last minute or having only half of the guests show up can result in a minor debacle, since the talent will still need to be paid in full. On the positive side, few things are more fun than a cozy night of carousing at home with the ladies!

- **Gypsy Gathering:** Hire a fortune-teller, astrologer, or tarot card reader. Get the bride a full thirty-minute reading and schedule the other guests for quick ten-minute sessions. Dim the lights, drape tapestries over the furniture, play some old Fleetwood Mac, and burn some incense while you channel spirits and see into the future.

- **Swedish Massage Soiree:** Hire a masseuse who makes house calls and travels with her own portable massage table. Complete the party by offering moisturizing facial masks and sliced cucumbers as eye refreshers, lighting scented candles, and serving refreshing drinks and healthful snacks. (Bloody Marys can be both at once!)

- **Henna Tattoo Night:** Hire an expert in this ancient art to adorn the hands and feet of the guests with intricate, gorgeous, and delicate tattoos. In traditional Indian custom, this beautification routine is performed on brides the night before their wedding, but here, the bridesmaids get the benefits, too! The temporary henna designs should wash off in several days, so they'll be gone before the ceremony if you hold your party weeks in advance. Be sure to have cameras on hand to capture the impressive designs.

Rite of Passage Revel

The highly noble goal of this fabulous, faux New Age party—which includes all kinds of delightful, hilarious at-home hazing activities—is to cleanse the bride of her checkered past, so she can get married with a clean slate! Whip up some healthful and refreshing drinks and let the purifications begin (wheatgrass shots optional).

Ex-Boyfriend Exorcism

Especially appropriate for the bride who took her "swinging single" years seriously, this rite is designed to lay the wandering spirits of the bride's old boyfriends to rest, so she can enter holy matrimony unfettered by the ghosts of the past. The key accessory is a bunch of dried sage. If your nearby New Age store, organic grocer, or florist is fresh out, try potent sage incense, widely available in stores.

   Appoint a mistress of ceremonies to take charge of the exorcism—any bridesmaid or maid of honor can play this part. She should know the names and a few pertinent details of the ex-boyfriends who need to be exorcised, and she should be willing to wear a black witchy gown or some sort of mystical headdress.

• Gather the bride and other ladies gather in a circle—the "Circle of Power"—while the mistress of ceremonies performs the ceremonial lighting of the sage (she should hold a match to the dried herb bundle until it just begins to smolder).

• Once the bouquet begins to let off its potent, magical smoke, the mistress of ceremonies should gesture to the north, south, east, and west, intoning this chant: "Through the ages, sage has been used to cleanse and renew the spirit, and we now call upon its special power to exorcise the spirits of the bride's ex-boyfriends." She can use these exact words, or she can make up something on the spot. But she shouldn't laugh! Ex-boyfriend exorcisms are very serious business.

- The mistress of ceremonies will then clearly state the name of the first ex-boyfriend, along with some identifying details—so the spirits will know who he is for sure. For example, she might say, "John, the least talented guitar player in the world, may your spirit be gone!" The Circle of Power will then repeat in unison, "John, begone!"

Note: If your group happens to have access to a fireplace or can find an open space to start a campfire, conduct the exorcism there. The spirits prefer it.

Top-Forty Chart Cleansing

Before the bride joins her CD collection everlastingly with his and embarks on a musically mature, married life, going through this rite of passage is essential—many brides have a lifetime of bad songs to get out of their systems! Rent a karaoke machine and have her belt out all the classics—from her favorite pop songs in sixth grade to the sentimental tunes that made her misty-eyed in high school. Not one drippingly sentimental ballad, cheesy rock song, or anything she might have slow-danced to in junior high should escape your playlist. (The printed inventory will be her treasured memento of her lifetime of musical gaffes!) She may pick one guest to join her at the microphone for each tune, and seeing who remembers which lyrics is as much fun as humming along! Bolster the singers with cold cocktails to soothe their sore throats. After this exhilarating evening, the bride will be ready to move forward into matrimony without all that bad musical baggage! Making a bootleg recording of the occasion is highly recommended.

Embarrassing Photo Purification

This event offers the bride an awesome, once-in-a-lifetime opportunity to remake history and rectify her bad image—by collecting all the unflattering photos that friends have taken of her over the years!

Before the party, tell everyone to find the most embarrassing photos of the bride in their possession—preferably one that also includes them. Before the bride arrives, have the guests paste the photograph in a special blank journal the hostess has bought for the occasion, and write a paragraph below the image that explains why they adore the bride, what was happening at that moment, and how much they treasure their friendship with her.

Hilarity will ensue when the bride pages through the book at the party. For extra fun, have guests read their own paragraphs aloud with the bride looking (and cringing) over their shoulder. At the end of the night, the bride retains the book as a keepsake—although the best part of the gift is definitely having those horrendous photos out of other people's hands! With this book in her possession— no doubt under lock and key—the bride can walk to the altar with her head held high. (Don't remind her that you still have the negatives.)

Fabulous Tip

THE BEST LAST-MINUTE BACHELORETTE GAME

Forget to come up with a game until the day before the bachelorette festivities? Change the Fabulous Bridal Quiz (see page 64) from a polite shower pastime to a daring bachelorette party game! Write questions that focus on the bride's wild past (and leave the groom, and other tame subjects, out of it). Include her junior high mishaps, funny dating faux pas, and legendary college exploits. The bridesmaids can debate over questions like, "What's the naughtiest thing the bride did on her twenty-first birthday?" while the bride decides whether to reveal the truth!

The Wedding Weekend

3

THE GOLDEN RULES

With far-flung friends and relatives flying in early, and festive dinners and intimate gatherings being held in the days before the ceremony, the wedding "day" has become the wedding weekend. Even if you live right next door to the ceremony site, your schedule in the days before the wedding will likely be jam-packed. At the very least, you will attend the rehearsal dinner the evening before the ceremony, and there may be an "afterglow" event to attend the following day. For a destination wedding on an exotic island or rustic farm, the timeline can expand to four or five days. You'll need stamina, as well as stunning social skills, to survive the marathon in style. Follow these golden rules and you'll give the performance of a lifetime.

Be Bold

Once upon a time, bridesmaids just stood around looking pretty— but these days, they have to be up for a challenge! You might be asked to help row an outrigger canoe between tropical islands to the ceremony, or the group might be asked to wear matching outfits and ski halfway down a mountain to the wedding site. Or, the reception might be so large that you feel like Evita when you give your speech onstage in front of hundreds of people! Whatever the challenge, go for the gold. You're not just a supportive friend wearing a questionable out-fit—you're the bride's fellow adventurer!

Let Love Rule

Don't bottle up your emotions! Whether you shed tears during the ceremony or broadcast your love for the happy couple over the microphone at the reception, let your sentimental side show. Weddings are the one place where everybody gets to be as sappy, syrupy, and romantic as they want. It's beautiful. Go with it!

Hydrate, Hydrate, Hydrate

Down at least one full glass of water between each festive glass of cham-pagne or wine, and stay within your comfort zone—the sobriety level you might aim for at an office party—or, even more challenging, the level at which you'd feel comfortable chatting up a gorgeous movie star. The idea is to be dazzling, not dazed and confused.

Nail the Timing

If you are a punctual person, fabulous! If not, buck up and be prompt, whether it's for the wedding procession or your own speech. Being on time is one way of showing the bride—and everyone else—how much you love and respect her.

Obey the Twenty-Four-Hour Rule

In the twenty-four-hour period preceding the wedding, insulate the bride from stress at all costs. If you are irritated or concerned about something and you feel you must get it off your chest, talk to another bridesmaid about what's eating you. Don't hassle the bride, have it out with her, or disturb her in any way once the time-honored gag rule goes into effect. In addition to being a kind and generous friend in these last hours, be willing to do some extra work—smoothing things over with the caterer or calming down the bride's mother—so the bride can enjoy her exhilarating day to the hilt.

THE GREAT DATE DEBATE

There are many compelling reasons to bring a date with you to a wedding. Some stem from romantic sentiments—it's great to hold hands during those emotional speeches—while others are more practical, like needing someone to pal around with when everyone else couples up. But before you grab the first guy you see, consider the benefits of going alone—flying solo is liberating and much better than bringing an undesirable date.

THE BIG PICTURE

As a bridesmaid, you will busy at bridal headquarters—so if your companion doesn't have the energy or will to tackle the social situations alone, he or she might be better left at home! Also, if your date doesn't know the couple getting married, he or she may feel out of place at such an intimate occasion, given that you will be MIA much of the time.

The date debate will be moot, however, if you are not supposed to bring anyone at all. If you are in doubt, the first place to look is the wedding invitation: your name *and* your steady's name (or the words "and guest") should appear on the envelope. If not, you may be expected to fly solo. Fortunately, if you have a serious, live-in significant other, this probably won't be an issue. The protocol these days is to invite significant others, and some brides even emphasize their importance by seating them with you at the bridal table.

But what about your new crush? Again, check your invite. If it doesn't specify "and guest" or "plus one," you might be out of luck. If your date is extremely important to you, discuss the issue with the bride—but know that adding one more person to the guest list may mean that the bride has to bump someone she cherishes. Proceed with caution.

quiz

WILL HE BE A GREAT DATE OR A DOWNRIGHT DISASTER?

There are certain kinds of men who make perfect wedding dates for bridesmaids, and there are certain kinds of men who are nothing but a liability at a wedding. The question is not whether you have a date to bring, but whether you want to bring him at all! Use the quiz that follows to determine whether the man you have in mind will be a fabulous date or a complete flop.

The (platonic) friend who agrees to be your date probably has the following ulterior motive:

a ⸰ Scoring some free food and drinks.

b ⸰ Hitting on the hot single girls.

c ⸰ None—he just wants to be a good friend to you.

When you tell him that, as a bridesmaid, you won't be able to spend much time with him, his attitude could be described as

a ⸰ Perturbed—he wonders aloud what the hell he's going to do with a bunch of strangers for an entire weekend.

b ⸰ Zoned out—he seems to think it won't make a difference one way or another.

c ⸰ Supportive—he intuitively understands your commitment to the bride and starts listing the things he can do during the day while you're at the salon.

The day the wedding invitation arrives in the mail, his reaction is to

a ⸰ Demand to know why you seem excited, since you've already been to two weddings this year.

b ⸗ Ask if you'll pay for the hotel room, since the bride is *your* friend.

c ⸗ Give you a big kiss and appear nearly as thrilled about attending the event as you are.

The last time you went to a wedding with him, what sticks out in your mind is

a ⸗ How he complained about the game he had to miss to attend the ceremony.

b ⸗ How he got wasted and embarrassed you at the reception.

c ⸗ How he held your hand tightly during the ceremony and looked at you adoringly afterward.

If you and your date were mistaken for a married couple at the event, he would

a ⸗ Wait for you to clarify the situation while looking around the room like a trapped rat.

b ⸗ Raise his eyebrows sarcastically and say, "Riiiight."

c ⸗ Smile charmingly and say, "She hasn't deemed me worthy."

S C O R I N G : **1 point for every a, 2 points for every b, and 3 points for every c**

5–8 points ⸗ **Anxious Guy**

He is in some major denial about matrimony and tends to trivialize the depth and poignancy of weddings out of an irrational fear of losing his bachelor status. If you see him for who he is—a guy trying to resist the social pressure he feels to get married before he's totally ready—he can be a great date. As long as he knows that you view the wedding as a fabulous party instead of an excuse to air your desire for a lifelong commitment, he can be a fabulous laugh-a-minute date who really knows how to have fun.

8–12 points ⸘ Big Liability

This guy can make even the most fun wedding seem like a long weekend in hell (and not only that, he's so unreliable that he might back out at the last minute). Better to fly solo than be dragged down by this undesirable date. Even if you will be the only bridesmaid at the wedding without a man at your side, embrace your single status!

12–15 points ⸘ Chivalrous Stud

He will charm the bride and her family, provide the emotional support you need, twirl you around the dance floor when the time comes, and, best of all, allow you all the room you need to pay attention to the bride. Whether he is your full-time steady or your longtime friend, this guy is a complete winner, the perfect date to bring to your best friend's wedding. Just be careful—if you're not really interested in him, be sure you send that message loud and clear.

Still stumped? Try the bonus round:

The only man at the wedding you can imagine wanting to be alone with is

a ⸘ The great guy you brought as a date.

b ⸘ Your gorgeous ex-boyfriend who will also be there. (It's bad, but you love to be bad.)

c ⸘ Whoever appeals, because your date certainly doesn't.

(If you answered b or c, ditch your date.)

WORD ALERT
. . . .
⸘ SAFETY DATE ⸘

This is a term for a person with whom you have established a completely platonic relationship, based on simple friendship (or mutual social survival) rather than romance. The beauty of the safety date is that there are no flying sparks to stamp out, no hurt feelings, and no awkward moments—just plenty of socially sanctioned time together! A real safety date is someone to treasure and treat well. There is also the *Denial Safety Date*—someone with whom you pretend to share a platonic friendship, but who actually carries a torch for you. This situation can be emotionally trying and is essentially a hassle.

TRAVEL SAVVY

Where you stay and what's in your suitcase can make or break your wedding weekend—so take these travel tips to heart before you board a plane or book a room.

WHERE TO STAY

A bridesmaid's bedroom or hotel room is her beautification center and her headquarters for hangover healing. Unfortunately, decent lodging doesn't come cheap, but doing some minor damage to your bank account is worth it when your sanity hangs in the balance. Review these handy lists of lodging options before you take the reservation plunge, and then choose the place where you'll wake up feeling bold, beautiful, righteous, relaxed, and ready to party!

Luxury Hotel

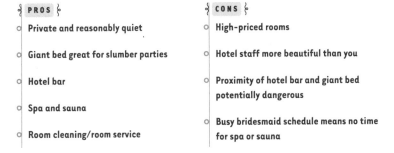

PROS	CONS
Private and reasonably quiet	High-priced rooms
Giant bed great for slumber parties	Hotel staff more beautiful than you
Hotel bar	Proximity of hotel bar and giant bed potentially dangerous
Spa and sauna	Busy bridesmaid schedule means no time for spa or sauna
Room cleaning/room service	

Advice: Ask for a quiet room. Try to share with other bridesmaids to bring down the cost.

Classy Bed-and-Breakfast

❧ PROS ❧	❧ CONS ❧
Pleasant, homey atmosphere	Expensive rooms
Quiet in the evenings	Noisy in the morning—the *very early* morning
Brownie points scored with the bride's mother ("My spinster aunt Penelope is staying there, too!")	Unavoidable small talk with owners and other guests
Fabulous breakfast included	Allergens in the environment due to ancient stuffed furniture or pets
	Lack of privacy due to paper-thin walls and nosy guests

Advice: Bring allergy medication and earplugs.

Cheesy Motel

❧ PROS ❧	❧ CONS ❧
Cheap rooms	Appearance of being financially challenged, unemployed, or both
No morning small talk with other wedding guests (you'll be the only wedding guest staying there)	Scratchy polyester-blend sheets; bad fluorescent lighting in bathroom; depressing, pea-sized outdoor pool
Rooms always available, even when everywhere else is booked	High likelihood that your neighbors will have loud, late-night sex
Rowdiness in the halls and rooms unlikely to be checked, so you could host a party	Possibility of car getting vandalized in dimly lit parking lot

Advice: If you're driving, bring a pillow and other comforts of home.

Camping

PROS

- Free!

- Opportunity to experience the beauty of nature

- Great excuse for not being perfectly made up and well coiffed

- Will please your outdoorsy or budget-conscious date

CONS

- Dark under-eye circles from restless night spent listening to deer/raccoons/ bears prowl around the tent

- No decent shower

- Uncomfortable sleeping arrangements preclude cuddling with outdoorsy date

- Nightlong proximity to campfires might make you a barbecue-scented bridesmaid

Advice: Arrange to get ready for the wedding in another bridesmaid's hotel room.

WHAT TO PACK

With this ultimate never-get-caught-unprepared packing list, you'll be physically and psychically prepared for the wedding weekend.

What to Pack . . . and Why

Products from your bathroom at home
If the hotel soap gives you an allover body rash, you'll still have to wear your sleeveless bridesmaid dress.

Cozy pajamas
You won't get much sleep, but you can make those few hours count by being comfortable.

Fabulous rehearsal dinner outfit
This is your chance to show everyone how divine you can look when the bride isn't choosing your clothes.

Bridesmaid dress, shoes, accessories
You have no choice.

Great lipstick and sparkly hair accessories
They might distract people from your bad bridesmaid dress.

Shawl or wrap
Borrowing his tuxedo jacket when it gets cold will make your outfit look even worse.

Expansive outfit for the trip home

You'll need something large to wear in the event of cake- or hangover-induced bloating.

Shoes

Bring at least one comfy pair to change into.

Sunscreen

If you protect your skin now, you'll still look fabulous when you're fifty.

Allergy medicine

Runny noses aren't cute.

Ibuprofen or painkiller of choice

Unless you successfully observe Golden Rule number 3 (Hydrate, Hydrate, Hydrate), you'll need it for your hangover.

Wedding invitation and directions

Being late or lost will ruin your cool.

Camera

You'll want to get photos of yourself chatting with handsome, well-dressed men, or capture the image of your boyfriend well dressed for once.

ALSO BRING AN EMERGENCY REPAIR KIT: needle and thread, baby wipes for removing lipstick stains from cheeks, bandages for foot blisters, tissues, cotton swabs, eyedrops for taking the red out of eyes and last-minute skin flaws, clear nail polish, colored nail polish that matches your manicure or pedicure, extra stockings

The Wedding Gift

Thanks to the excellent rules of etiquette, there's no need to lug a wedding present in your suitcase—you officially have up to a year after the wedding to send the gift! If the wedding expenses have depleted your bank account, this rule permits you to recover financially before choosing the gift. Take the time! Your choice of a wedding present shouldn't be influenced by stress about being over your budget.

Don't feel compelled to purchase something lavish—even if you know that the other bridesmaids are dropping a fortune. Aim to spend somewhere between fifty and one hundred fifty dollars. Remember that any heartfelt offering will be welcomed! Another excellent solution to financial woes is to go in on the wedding gift with others—buying something expensive and memorable is easier when several people share the cost. You may also choose to purchase a wedding gift off the registry.

There is no excuse for neglecting to send your gift within the allotted year—ignore those pesky rumors that say bridesmaids are exempt from giving wedding gifts because of their previous expenditures, such as the dress. Even a small gift can show how much you care. For a traditional Jewish wedding, for example, you could give seven small, inexpensive gifts, each representing one of the seven traditional Jewish marriage blessings.

For indecisive bridesmaids, a gift certificate provides the perfect solution—particularly when you are close to the bride but not as well acquainted with the groom. Dinner for two at their favorite restaurant, a pair of theater or sporting-event tickets, or an overnight stay at a romantic bed-and-breakfast gives the couple the opportunity for an intimate evening together.

THE REHEARSAL DINNER

The essentials of the rehearsal and the accompanying dinner—a walk-through of the ceremony and a meal afterward—haven't changed a great deal over the decades, but the emphasis has. These days, the meal is often given more importance than the actual wedding rehearsal. The dinner has become such an important and lavish part of the wedding weekend that the hosting duties have changed hands: in the old days, the bride's family was responsible for the rehearsal dinner as well as the wedding, but more recently it has become customary for the dinner to be hosted by the groom's parents.

THE BIG PICTURE

The guest list is usually kept small, to provide an opportunity for the bride and groom to spend quality time with their intimate circle of friends and family. The time is especially important for close relatives of the couple who live far away and won't have other chances to visit. At more casual weddings, the exclusive guest list is often dispensed with and everyone who arrives in town the night before the ceremony is invited. In such cases, the evening often involves dinner

WORD ALERT

. . . .

❧ THE ROAST ❧

No, this is not a friendly campfire singalong with chocolate bars and marshmallows. This is part of the speech you may be giving at any point during the wedding festivities—one designed to secure some laughs while gently skewering the bride's more "distinctive" characteristics. Go for the "PG-13" rating when you roast. Stories about her ex-boyfriends or amusing sexual exploits are definitely not appropriate.

USAGE: The groom's father says good-naturedly, "I can't wait to hear you roast her!"

only—perhaps a barbecue or picnic; the rehearsal is then conducted the following morning, before the ceremony.

Rehearsal dinners often have the laid-back, casual feeling of an intimate family gathering, but etiquette is still an important component of the evening. The following overview of rehearsal dinner protocol puts all the necessary information at your fingertips. Follow these guidelines for good behavior, and you will win the award for most mannerly bridesmaid.

During the Rehearsal

The rabbi, minister, priest, or justice of the peace who will be performing the ceremony (or possibly the wedding coordinator) will tell your wedding party how to form the procession, walk up the aisle, and where to stand. If you are the maid of honor, the bride may practice handing you a simulated bouquet during the mock ceremony and retrieving it at the end. Normally, the vows aren't spoken, so the rehearsal probably won't take long. You will also be shown how to pair up and walk down the aisle in the recession.

Be alert and listen carefully so the ceremony will run smoothly the following day. (No giggling, chatting, or meditating over that hot guy/professional connection/old friend who will be attending the wedding!) Often, the rehearsal is tucked into the early afternoon so it won't interfere with the cocktail hour or dinner. Know the scheduled time in advance and be as punctual as possible!

During the Cocktail Hour

Dress appropriately. This event can range from pearls-and-heels formal to shorts-and-sandals casual—and you don't want to arrive wearing the wrong outfit! Do some research by asking the bride and other guests what they'll be wearing, and then dress to impress.

Show a high level of engagement, enthusiasm, and interest in other people. Being a bridesmaid provides you with an automatic reason to introduce yourself and break the ice with strangers. Make it your goal to find out how every person in the room knows the bride. Talk to elderly guests, children, anyone who seems shy or lonely, and anyone who speaks another language. If there are extraterrestrials in the crowd, speak with them, too.

Make thoughtful introductions. The crowd should be small compared to the wedding reception, and you will probably know enough folks to be able to make a few introductions. Get that medical student talking to the emergency-room doctor! This is the way bonding happens. When people get well acquainted at this event, the wedding day will be more relaxed and fun for everyone.

During the Dinner

Mind your manners! When you're a bridesmaid, people notice you. Elderly family members flying completely beneath your radar will not only know your name, age, and dating status, they will probably watch to make sure you behave appropriately at the table. Whether the meal involves a serve-yourself buffet or four-star service, chew with your mouth closed, place your silverware neatly on your plate when you're finished, and always keep your conversation polite.

Do not, repeat, do *not* allow yourself to get rip-roaring drunk. Imagine what might happen if you got so drunk at the rehearsal dinner that your uncontrollable hangover the following day compelled you to throw up right before or during the wedding. Then imagine that this has actually happened to more than one well-meaning bridesmaid.

Be gracious. The bride and groom often take the opportunity at the rehearsal dinner to thank their bridesmaids and groomsmen by presenting them with their gifts, if they haven't already done so at an earlier occasion. Accept the gift politely and thank the bride cordially.

During Your Speech

You'll see all the dos and don'ts of public speaking committed at this event, since it's generally the time that the floor is entirely open for any guest to take the microphone. Don't let yourself become a *don't*. Prepare in advance by reading Tips for Spectacular Speeches and Triumphant Toasts (see page 112).

There is a preferred order for rehearsal dinner speeches, so wait your turn to take the microphone. The hosts—usually the groom's parents—should be the first to welcome guests by raising their glass. According to etiquette, the sentiment should then be returned by the bride's parents. When these formalities are over, anyone can jump in.

Word Alert

. . . .

{ CHAMPAGNE }

Although this traditional wedding libation is delightfully light and excessively drinkable—and the French region where the grapes originate is pretty and picturesque—there are few darker or more difficult things than a champagne hangover. Sadly, they are too easily acquired! Since champagne is often served before the reception meal begins—when it will go straight to your head—the hangover risk factor at weddings is high. It is said that knowledge is power. Consider yourself in the know.

Spectacular Speeches and Triumphant Toasts

Think of it this way: that wedding crowd will applaud no matter what you say. OK, your toast should definitely honor the bride and groom—but the point is that you shouldn't feel compelled to be supremely witty, romantic, clever, poetic, or anything else that doesn't come naturally. Keeping your voice steady and standing up straight (without fidgeting) in front of a crowd is difficult enough, but it gets even harder if you don't feel totally comfortable with the content of your speech. Being confident is arguably the most important part of public speaking—so if you enjoy being funny, by all means be funny, but if you want to be serious, that's fabulous, too.

If you are the maid of honor, you may give a speech at the rehearsal dinner *and* at the wedding reception. The bride will usually give you advance warning if she expects you to speak at the reception. Bridesmaids who wish to make a toast generally do so at the rehearsal dinner, although, depending on the bride's wishes and the reception schedule, they may also do so at the wedding.

Making a wonderful, touching, and entertaining toast takes work. Speaking on the spur of the moment may sound great during those weeks of procrastination before the wedding, but the stress you'll experience as the time gets closer just isn't worth it. Besides, speeches given without some advance preparation often seem to ramble. The best way to alleviate your anxiety is to brainstorm ideas early and practice in private. Follow these practical tips to deliver an unforgettable toast.

○ **Contextualize your connection to the bride.** Without getting into boring details, mention how long you've known her, how you met, and some significant detail of your friendship.

○ Touch on why you love her so much, what makes her special, and why you feel honored to be speaking at her wedding.

○ Compliment the groom. If you know him well, this should be easy. If you don't know him well, focus on his accomplishments: "Leave it to Stacy to find a man who went to culinary school, can fix any problem on a car, and serenades her with his guitar at night." You can also talk about the ways he makes her happy. If you're at a loss, ask the bride for her ideas— and at least a couple of them should be tame enough for family to hear.

- Wish them a long and happy life together.

- Be heartfelt but not long-winded.

- Do some research. If you can't find the right words, find a poem or quote that expresses your feelings for you.

- Don't fidget. Hold the microphone with one hand and keep the other one at your side, until it is time to pick up your glass to toast the couple.

- Visualize the situation in advance. Will you be speaking to forty people or four hundred? Will you be standing on stage with a microphone or speaking from your assigned table? Having a good idea of the particulars will help you avoid bridesmaid-in-the-headlights syndrome. Don't worry about memorizing every last word of the speech—using notes is perfectly acceptable as long as you also make eye contact with the crowd.

- Try not to denigrate your speech by making negative comments about it afterward, even if your voice was shaking or you forgot part of it and ad-libbed badly. The point is not to draw attention to yourself, but to celebrate your friend, the bride, by always trying your best.

- Since rehearsal dinners are generally more intimate and casual than weddings, bridesmaids sometimes take the opportunity to do something more elaborate than a toast, such as getting together to perform a hilarious skit, or giving a slide show of the bride and groom as kids. Be sure the hosts are amenable before you plan something creative.

Fabulous Tip

HOW TO AVOID FEELING HUMILIATED ABOUT YOUR SPEECH

It is very likely that your speech will be recorded on the wedding videotape—and as one of the bride's closest friends, you will have to watch her wedding video eventually. Many bridesmaids describe the speech-viewing experience as excruciating! Unless you're looking to become a serious toastmaster and want tips on improving your performance, or you feel absolutely fine about watching yourself in the act of public speaking, you might try to avoid this unfortunate event. Rather than squirming on the bride's sofa, simply excuse yourself to refresh your drink or visit the bathroom when you sense the moment of doom approaching. The other option? Stick around and have a hearty laugh at your own expense.

THE WEDDING DAY AND THE RECEPTION

For every bride, no matter how formal her ceremony and reception, relaxed and fun-loving bridesmaids, personal gifts, and heartfelt toasts will always be better than the stuffy versions. If the bride has an attack of stress, don't take it personally. Instead, stay organized, be resourceful, try to think of possible solutions, and keep that crucial sense of humor intact—all part of being a good assistant. This section gives hints for bringing luck to the couple on their big day, breaks down the wedding-day schedule, dives into the juicy details of reception party protocol, demystifies the dancing, and gives all the guidelines for tackling your duties efficiently—so you can relax and have fun.

LUCKY CHARMS FOR THE NEWLYWEDS

The only lucky charms most bridesmaids will get on the morning of the wedding are the variety that come in a cereal bowl—but for the couple getting hitched, there are many cherished customs that will supposedly bring them good fortune. Bridesmaids frequently provide the bride with these talismans, so check out the summary of popular customs below and contribute the charm that fits her best!

Something Blue

Even the most practical bride—the one who since girlhood has been unmoved by superstitions, astrology, or fortune-telling—might adhere to the traditional good-luck custom of wearing "something old, something new, something borrowed, and something blue" for her wedding. And why not? This good-luck charm covers all the bases: new and old are worn together to ease the transition from the old life to the new one; the borrowed item, preferably lent by a happily married woman, is worn for good luck; and the blue item represents fidelity. Some lucky brides borrow sapphires from relatives to wear, but those who don't have access to fabulous jewels will appreciate receiving a sentimental blue item from her bridesmaids as a gift. This can be given at the shower, at the bachelorette party, or even on the day of the wedding. Here are some traditional and not-so-traditional ideas:

- **The classic blue garter**

- **Tiny blue cornflowers for the bride's hair**

- **Aquamarine cocktail ring**

- **Delicate wrist bangles**

- **A temporary blue tattoo (for the groom's eyes only)**

- **Pedicure with blue polish (hidden under closed-toe shoes)**

- **Blue lingerie (in a shade that won't show through the wedding dress)**

- **A strip of blue ribbon to pin inside the hem of her wedding gown**

Confetti

According to Italian tradition, *confètti*—the Italian word for sugarcoated almonds—represent the combined bitterness and sweetness in married life. The tasty treats are often wrapped in tulle, tied with a ribbon, and distributed at weddings. For the maid of honor or bridesmaid who wants to help the bride make simple wedding favors, these sweet bundles are easy to assemble and affordable to make, and they bring a lovely, traditional touch to any wedding celebration.

Throwing Rice

Rice was originally thrown at couples departing their weddings to encourage them to be fruitful and multiply. These days, people more often throw rose petals, and at some weddings, guests even hold glittering sparklers to light the way from the church or reception to the getaway car. Whatever the chosen token, the happy intent of showering newlyweds with good wishes as they depart remains the same. The rose petals or other tokens should be distributed by the maid of honor and bridesmaids before the couple's departure, so everyone can say "au revoir" in style.

Decorating the Newlyweds' Getaway Car

Shoes are no longer tied to or thrown at the newlyweds' getaway vehicle for luck, but the tradition of decorating the getaway car is still going strong! Although the groomsmen often initiate this event, bridesmaids might share in the decorating duties or even take charge if the guys don't get on the ball. Whether you scrawl the traditional "Just Married" across the back windshield and tie cans to the bumper, or go with something more inventive, like stringing fresh flower garlands on the outside of the car and draping the inside with sweet-smelling blossoms, the couple will be delighted by the unexpected surprise.

Fabulous Tip

HOW TO FEEL LIKE A SUPERHERO IN YOUR BRIDESMAID DRESS

If you're forced to wear a ferociously unflattering dress, you may actually be saving your best friend's life, at least according to old traditions. The custom of the couple surrounding themselves with similarly dressed friends stems from the belief that evil spirits might wish to harm the bride and groom— and having everyone dressed alike was thought to confuse those unruly phantoms. So the scarier your dress is, the faster those spirits will scurry for cover. You've got the power! (If only the job came with that invisible airplane.)

Two Must-Have Checklists

Despite months of preparation, even the most organized wedding day can dissolve into hilarity and chaos as ceremony time approaches—but instead of getting flustered, hold up your end of the deal. Stay on top of your job with these checklists, which delineate your wedding-day duties.

Checklist One: How to Be a Fabulous Bridesmaid

In the morning, pull together the makeup, hair accessories, jewelry, bridesmaid dress, and any other things you'll need in order to primp and get fabulous, then head over to bridal headquarters—usually a private room at the wedding site or the bride's hotel suite. (Maid of honor, bring that crib sheet for your toast, if you're giving one.)

- Organize breakfast or lunch for the bride and the bridesmaids on the wedding day, if it seems that, between beauty appointments and other details, eating sensibly has escaped the bride's mind. (She should eat *before* she gets dressed, so no food stains mar her gown—and the same goes for the bridesmaids.)

- Be helpful and run last-minute errands for the bride. Help her get dressed, then dress yourself, and make the necessary makeup and hair adjustments.

- Cover your face (and the bride's) with a pillowcase when pulling the gowns over your heads so no makeup ends up where it doesn't belong.

- Maid of honor, be sure the bouquets and bridesmaids are in order.

- Before you get in that limousine to go to the wedding site, pack your purse with the reception essentials—

a cashmere wrap in case it gets cold, your fabulous lipstick, and breath mints. Don't leave it in the car in all the excitement! (Maid of honor, be sure the bride gives you the groom's ring before you leave for the wedding.)

- If for some reason you end up needing to dress separately and are under your own steam to get to the wedding site, arrive at least thirty minutes before the ceremony starts.

- Be on time for photographs! They'll probably take place before and/or directly after the ceremony, at the ceremony or reception site.

- Maid of honor, put that precious gold circle on your thumb for safekeeping.

- Take your place for the procession (as practiced at the rehearsal).

- When the music or other signal is given, begin the procession. Walk slowly!

Fan out during the ceremony in your prearranged positions, and stay at attention.

Maid of honor, take the bride's bouquet and offer the ring at just the right moment.

Walk back down the aisle in the recession (as practiced at the rehearsal), congratulate the newlyweds, and get ready to party at the reception! (Don't forget the post-ceremony photo session or receiving line, if one is planned.)

Checklist Two: How to Be a Fabulous Friend

Put those official duties and ceremony details aside for a moment—this little list is about making the bride feel cherished and loved! On the morning of the wedding, take a moment to appreciate your bond with the bride, and give the gift of your friendship all day long. Show the bride how much you love and appreciate her in the small ways that matter. Use these ideas for inspiration—and let your natural friendship intuition be your guide.

Be the bride's jester and soothe her jitters.

Act like you know what you're doing.

Just be around—a lot!

Ask her if she needs anything.

Keep her excited and keep her smiling.

Reassure her if she gets commitment jitters at the last minute.

Remind her of the wonderful things about her relationship with the groom.

Don't hate her for making you look like an overstuffed Barbie doll, or for marrying a man you think isn't perfect for her, or for anything else.

Remember that in doing all of these things, you are cementing the foundation of a fabulous lifelong friendship.

◦ IN THE RIBBONS ◦

This phrase has nothing to do with the bridesmaids doing a Maypole dance, thankfully. In fact, it has nothing to do with bridesmaids at all—but you should know that it means a special honor section in the seating set aside for immediate family, generally the first few rows, which are traditionally marked by ribbons or bows.

USAGE: The bride's mother says, "Why didn't that usher seat Grandma Bessie in the ribbons?"

GETTING DOWN THE AISLE IN STYLE

There are as many different types of weddings as there are religious beliefs, all of which have distinctive and delightful ceremonies and rites. In the United States, where Judaism, Protestantism, and Catholicism are the three most widely practiced faiths, the main events are the procession, the ceremony, and the recession. If you are involved in a wedding where the customs are unfamiliar to you, don't hesitate to admit ignorance and ask questions. The more you know about the meanings of the rituals at the wedding, the more meaningful the ceremony will be to you.

Generally, the ushers lead the procession, followed by junior ushers or bridesmaids, if they are in the party. Bridesmaids are next down the aisle—either walking in pairs or in single file—and the maid of honor follows. If there is a flower girl or ring bearer, she or he immediately precedes the bride, who walks accompanied by her choice of attendant (in Christian weddings, often

her father; in Jewish weddings, both her father and mother). A bride may also choose to walk with another relative, such as a grandparent, or with the groom, or she may even choose to walk down the aisle alone. All of these options are perfectly acceptable according to etiquette and generally won't affect the order of the bridesmaids and the maid of honor, who precede the bride in the procession.

In Jewish weddings, the rabbi waits for the bride and groom under a *huppah*, or flowered canopy, which symbolizes the home that the couple will share. Slight variations in the order of the procession and recession, and in the standing arrangements at the altar are common. To nail your role in the real event, attend the formal rehearsal and follow these simple tips for cruising the wedding catwalk without tripping up.

○ **Don't lock your knees or hold your breath while walking down the aisle.**

○ **Once the bride reaches the altar, if you're the maid of honor, fluff her dress and make it look pretty.**

○ **Avoid feeling extremely self-conscious (it can lead to the above-mentioned dreaded knee-locking situation) by remembering that the guests are only watching you out of politeness. The second after you walk by, you'll be totally forgotten as everyone cranes their neck to see the bride.**

○ **Keep a natural expression. Whether you look serious or sport an ear-to-ear smile, do your best to avoid looking forced. Try not to roll your eyes, even if that baby in the crowd won't stop screaming, or make any other suspect facial expression.**

○ **Hold your bouquet high. It sounds silly, but bouquets can be surprisingly heavy, so don't let your arms sag and the** flowers droop, even if the ceremony goes on forever. That goes double for the maid of honor, who holds the bride's bouquet as well as her own when the bride and groom exchange rings.

O Enjoy the moment when the couple says the vows—the best part of being a bridesmaid is being close enough to see the emotions cross their faces.

O If you really lose it and start crying uncontrollably, start counting the number of bad outfits or tacky hairdos in the audience, which will allow you to look lovingly at the crowd and be distracted from the big emotional reasons for your tears.

O Wait for the prearranged signal to start the recession down the aisle. In Jewish ceremonies, the groom crushes a wineglass beneath his feet at the end of the ceremony, directly before the recession.

WORD ALERT

· ·

❨ REVERENCE ❩

(used as a verb) **Depending on the denomination, and the preference of the minister, in certain religious ceremonies the wedding party may be asked to "reverence"—perform a short curtsy or slight bow in front of the altar—as part of the procession. If you do not wish to participate, either because you do not share the faith or simply feel uncomfortable with the ritual, you may politely ask to be excused from the task. Any minister worth his or her salt will respect this as your prerogative.**

USAGE: The minister says, "At the altar, please reverence."

CORRECT RESPONSE **(if you do not wish to participate):** "Do I have to reverence?"

THE GROOMSMAN GUIDE:
HOW TO HANDLE THAT GUY IN THE TUXEDO

Just as the maid of honor is paired with the best man at every possible moment, each bridesmaid is assigned a groomsman with whom to walk down the aisle and dance at the reception. (Maid of honor, you may be asked to speak at the reception, after the best man makes his toast—don't let him show you up!) Save your sanity by reading this handy chart, which will help you identify the kind of dude you're dealing with.

Ceremony

Debauched Bachelor	He behaves perfectly—it's that honor code thing.
Ironic Intellectual	He can't keep the I'll-never-get-married smirk off his face.
Groom's Younger Brother	He appears thoughtful. ("Which hot babe will I hit on at the reception?")
Granola Guy	He smiles and looks slightly dazed (as usual).
A+ Groomsman	He looks attentive and moved.

Dinner

Debauched Bachelor	He's too busy signaling for wine to have a conversation.
Ironic Intellectual	He's too busy making cynical comments to eat, but at least he's funny.

Groom's Younger Brother	If he's single, he tries to pick up the hot girls (watch out!).
Granola Guy	He picks at his mashed potatoes and asks if the caterers recycle.
A+ Groomsman	He amuses the whole table without monopolizing the conversation.

Speech

Debauched Bachelor	He makes you sound clever and funny!
Ironic Intellectual	He makes you sound dull and sentimental.
Groom's Younger Brother	He'll avoid complimenting his brother, so be sure you praise the groom in your speech.
Granola Guy	Make your speech funny if possible—his will be earnest.
A+ Groomsman	His awesome speech will be a hard act to follow. Come prepared!

Dance Floor

Debauched Bachelor	Watch your back: he likes to dirty dance.
Ironic Intellectual	He's too self-conscious to groove. You're the party starter.
Groom's Younger Brother	Goofball kid-type antics make him an embarrassing partner.
Granola Guy	He does the Birkenstock shuffle.
A+ Groomsman	He starts everyone doing the Hustle.

The Formal Photographs

Professional photographers are part of almost every wedding, and so are what might seem like endless rounds of posed shots. Before you get grumpy, remember that the bride and groom are paying big bucks to have this shutterbug catch them and their loved ones on the big day. Deal with the wet grass, try your best not to squint, and smile until it hurts! This is what friendship is about.

The posed group photographs are usually taken after the ceremony, often at the reception site, before the receiving line begins. Increasingly, however, couples are having them taken before the wedding, when everyone is at his or her most picture-perfect. Be sure you know when and where to show up with your smile. As in any endurance activity, caffeine will enhance your performance— and after the first fifty photos, you'll be glad to have the help.

During the reception, don't be tacky by trying to put yourself and your date in front of the lens at opportune moments. And even if you have taken advanced photography classes, refrain from pointing out great shots to the photographer. Would you want someone in a questionable dress telling you how to do your job? To act with supreme confidence and class, you might try behaving as if the clicking cameras and whirring camcorders weren't there at all. (Note: If you're single, check out the photographer's assistant—they are often very sexy individuals.)

The Receiving Line

The point of this tradition is to allow each guest a chance to personally greet the bride and groom at a large and formal wedding, where they might not otherwise get face time. Whether you are standing in the line or simply passing through it, always put down your glass or plate so you can greet people properly. At small, intimate ceremonies, the receiving line is often deemed unnecessary, since the couple will presumably have a chance to speak with everyone at the reception.

The line generally forms at the reception site, after the formal photographs, but it may take place at the church, directly after the ceremony. The bride will sometimes ask her bridesmaids to stand in the line, in which the order usually goes as follows: the bride's mother, the groom's mother, the bride, the groom, and then the bridesmaids. Fathers are not required to be there—as usual, they get off the hook—although they are absolutely welcome if they wish to stand in line. Stepparents usually only stand in the receiving line if they are particularly close to the bride or bridegroom. Sometimes, instead of standing in the receiving line, bridesmaids will preside over the guest book, encouraging people to sign when they have finished greeting the newlyweds and the family.

THE BRIDE'S TABLE

Bridesmaids always score when it comes to seating arrangements—no back-of-the-room, faraway table for you! Sometimes, the bridesmaids, ushers, and their significant others will be seated at the bride's table at the center of the room. In other cases, only the best man and maid of honor, along with the couple's parents, will be seated at the bride's table, with the rest of the wedding party seated at a nearby table.

Often, newlyweds choose to sit on their own, at a table for two, instead of having a bridal table. This makes it easier for them to circulate during the meal. (Some couples also do this to avoid having to exclude good friends who aren't in the wedding party from the high-status table.) In this situation, the wedding party will generally be seated together, near the bridal couple's table for two.

You'll know it's time for you to head to your seat when (a) the receiving line is finished and you see the bride and groom heading to their table; (b) someone gives a signal indicating that everyone should move to the dining area; or (c) you (and the cutie you're talking to) are suddenly the only people left at the prereception cocktail bar.

At the bride's table, the traditional seating arrangement is as follows: the maid of honor on the groom's left, the best man on the bride's right, with the other bridesmaids and ushers, and their significant others, on either side. Men and women usually alternate, and couples may be seated in a staggered manner, instead of next to each other, to mix things up and encourage socializing. Sometimes, the spouses and significant others of the wedding party can't be included at the bridal table because of lack of space. If this is the case, the attendant, whether married or not, must stay with the bridal party.

HOW TO SURVIVE THE BRIDESMAID'S CATWALK

Many large or formal wedding receptions are hosted by an official announcer who formally introduces the attendants to the wedding crowd, just before the dinner begins. This agonizing ritual goes as follows: An announcer will say your name over the PA—your signal to take a turn on the bridesmaid's catwalk, the central reception floor—and you will walk some specified distance, perhaps wave, and even turn. In addition to letting everyone take a good gander at your bad dress, you may have to endure clapping, which can have a stinging ring of sarcasm when you're sporting a terrible outfit. How to survive? Walk as quickly as possible without tripping, and comfort yourself afterward with a glass of champagne.

RECEPTION PARTY PROTOCOL

Once the receiving line breaks up, or when a signal is given by the host or wedding planner, folks will find their seats for the reception meal. Many a bridesmaid has seized this moment to visit the restroom or take a breather, not realizing that the start of the reception means the beginning of a whole new set of duties. In fact, the reception is where the maid of honor gives her toast, if she's been asked to give one, and where the bridesmaids must dance with their groomsmen. The best way to stay on top of your duties is to know when to raise your glass and when to step onto the dance floor.

Making Toasts

If the guests have assigned seats, the toasts begin once everyone has found their tables and the champagne or wine glasses are filled. The best man will rise to make the first toast to the couple.

If the meal is being served buffet style, without planned seating, the best man may gather the guests (and the wedding party) and make his short toast directly after the receiving line breaks up, or right before the guests begin to serve themselves. When the best man finishes his speech, other members of the bridal party may then propose toasts.

At a formal wedding, everyone rises for the toast except the bride and groom—although this isn't a hard-and-fast rule, so you might look around to see if other people are getting up before you jump to your feet.

At a casual wedding with an open floor for speeches, one member of the couple might receive more toasts than the other. If you notice the scales tipping in the bride's or the groom's favor, and you aren't otherwise scheduled to speak, jump up and honor the less-toasted individual.

If you know in advance that you will be giving a speech, don't wait until the last minute to plan it, or you might get shown up by the best man! Never underestimate the importance of giving a good toast. (See Spectacular Speeches and Triumphant Toasts, page 112.)

Dancing

The signal to start dancing generally comes from the disc jockey, the leader of the band, or a member of the wedding party. Traditionally, the dancing begins

after the first course and continues throughout the evening, although these days receptions differ greatly and there are many possible alternatives to this schedule. At many ceremonies, the music and dancing do not begin until after the meal is finished. With a traditional schedule, however, dancing will proceed as follows: First, the bride and groom dance together. Next, the parents join them on the dance floor—for example, the bride's father may cut in on the groom to dance with the bride, and then the groom may ask the bride's mother to dance. Then the bridal party is called to the dance floor and jumps into the mix—bridesmaids, dance with your ushers! After a few minutes, whoever is at the microphone will invite everyone onto the dance floor. Dancing and eating and drinking will continue until it is time to cut the cake.

Encourage guests to get up and dance! A packed dance floor will make the reception feel like a righteous party, and it will enable the bride and groom to leave the dance floor and mingle with other guests.

Fabulous Tip

HOW TO AVOID GETTING CRUSHED DURING CHAIR DANCING

The **hora** is an Israeli folk dance often performed at Jewish weddings, in which the guests hold hands and form a circle around the newlyweds, who are lifted up on chairs as the guests dance around them. Keeping the newlyweds—who hold a napkin between them to symbolize their new marriage bond—head and shoulders above the crowd is hard work, however! This tradition is so fun and high-spirited that you'll probably want to help hoist the couple, but stand back and let the big boys and girls do the work unless your biceps can compete. After the newlyweds have been sufficiently celebrated, the bride's parents are often hoisted up and paraded around as well.

Defensive Dancing, or How to Recognize Potentially Dangerous Partners

Unlike dance clubs or parties, where people often dance individually and only occasionally partner up for fun, people at weddings hit the dance floor as couples. Since men stopped being trained in formal ballroom dancing quite a while ago, this is an unfortunate situation, especially given that most women *naturally* dance better than most (straight) men. Every former bridesmaid knows that what goes down on the dance floor sometimes isn't pretty.

In your extra-special bridesmaid's outfit, you are easily recognizable and approachable, and many male guests will feel comfortable asking you to dance, simply because you are wearing The Dress. Being a bridesmaid doesn't oblige you to partner up with everyone who asks, but the sassy reception spirit will probably persuade you to take a twirl with folks you wouldn't pick out of the lineup on your own. The best way to avoid dance-floor disasters? Gauge his dancing before you grab his hand! Study up on these classifications so you know what to expect when you join him on the dance floor.

- **The Silly Ed Grimley:** With his swinging arms and legs akimbo, this guy will be fun if you're not worried about impressing anyone with your dancing skills. He won't make you look graceful, but he will make you laugh.

- **The Big-Footed Fumbler:** Off the dance floor, he's an average man wearing an unremarkable suit. He is difficult to spot until you see his moves—but by then it's too late, and you're just inches away from him, trying to sway to the music. He will probably be grateful if, after one song, you suggest heading to the bar for a refreshing drink.

- **The Lambada Lover:** Be sure you're ready for his hip-grinding style when you agree to be his partner—shy girls might want to steer clear. This guy's sexy moves draw the spotlight every time!

- **The Swinger:** He'll whip you around in twirls and dips that might make the room do the same—especially if you've downed a bit too much cake and champagne. If you have a strong stomach and enjoy a strong lead, however, some fast turns on the floor with this mover and shaker are good for a rush!

- **The Wizened Waltzer:** Follow his steps, and concentrate. The waltz is supposed to be easy, but with these old guys, your misstep could land him in the ER.

WORD ALERT

. . . .

♪ THE DOLLAR DANCE ♪

This custom originates from the Polish practice of having each guest pay to dance with the bride or groom at the reception—the money was intended to help the couple pay for their honeymoon. Divorced of its origins and conducted merely for monetary reasons, the event has now become popular at American weddings but is considered vulgar by most etiquette experts.

USAGE: The bride says, "What do you think of us doing that dollar-dance thing? It's such a great way to come up with quick cash!"

CORRECT RESPONSE: "I think holding a car wash would be a better idea."

Formality Chart: Oh, Behave!

Knowing the level of formality of the wedding is an important step toward being the best bridesmaid you can be. At black-tie weddings, your party protocol should be informed by some etiquette, while at totally casual ceremonies you can check the stiff manners at the door. Use these benchmarks to figure out how to behave.

Profanity at Dinner

Black Tie Optional	Utter the words only among bridesmaids and make sure nobody else hears you.
Casual	You can get away with saying anything if you whisper.
Antiestablishment Love Fest	Let the Establishment have it!

Bra

Black Tie Optional	Wear it, or someone's mother might faint.
Casual	Don't bother. Use duct tape if necessary.
Antiestablishment Love Fest	Fly free.

Eyebrow Wax

Black Tie Optional	Just do it.
Casual	Sure, if you like the hot wax experience.
Antiestablishment Love Fest	Give the money to Amnesty International.

Bikini Wax

. . . .

Black Tie Optional   If it helps your peace of mind,
                                go for it.

Casual   Naked hot tubbing happens.

Antiestablishment Love Fest Naked hot tubbing happens—with
                                the lights off.

Job Networking

. . . .

Black Tie Optional   Bring your business cards.

Casual   Bring your business cards, but
                                leave them in the car.

Antiestablishment Love Fest Use your business cards as
                                coasters.

Taking Off Your Pumps

. . . .

Black Tie Optional   Keep your feet under wraps.

Casual   Slip them off under the table.

Antiestablishment Love Fest Dance barefoot. (Once the shoes
                                go, anything might be next.)

Flirting with the Help

. . . .

Black Tie Optional   Think *Dirty Dancing*. Fun, but
                                some folks might think it's a
                                no-no.

Casual   Sidle up to that sexy bartender.
                                Why not?

Antiestablishment Love Fest Observe equal opportunity
                                partying.

DAMAGE CONTROL:
HOW TO HANDLE OTHER PEOPLE'S BAD BEHAVIOR

Weddings, like holidays, wouldn't be true celebrations without a little bad behavior. This is no reflection on the bride or groom, but simply a fact of life: People misbehave at weddings. Prepare yourself for the worst by acquainting yourself with some of the most common poor behavior—and learn exactly how to respond in the fashion most befitting a fabulous bridesmaid.

The After-School Special

The recent divorce between the bride's parents is making things tense. The groom's father brought his latest floozy girlfriend to the ceremony, and the groom's mother is offended. The bride's older sister just announced her divorce the day before the ceremony. Let's face it: Weddings are supposed to be about families coming together in the name of love, but sometimes the love just isn't there, and every conceivable moment feels potentially explosive.

BE PREPARED TO

Smile constantly and defuse dangerous conversations by introducing totally neutral topics. For example, "Doesn't the wedding cake look lovely?"

The Me! Me! Me!

A family member or friend gives a self-referential toast that barely refers to the bride and groom, for example, "Marriage makes me think of my ex-spouse/ coming out/first love affair." This is particularly likely to come from a "black sheep" in the family.

BE PREPARED TO

Respond just as you would to anyone else's speech, by clapping or smiling or raising your glass—as long as everyone else does it—even if the person's words seemed completely offensive to you. Don't speak your judgment aloud. It's impossible to know right away whether the relatives found the toast atrocious; behavior that some people find utterly shocking is perfectly acceptable to others.

The "Annie" Syndrome

A willful child is allowed to run wild at the reception because his or her parents are too busy partying (or making out in the garden) to rein the child in. This scene can cause near-fatal disruptions on the dance floor, distract from the ceremonial cake cutting, and generally disturb the bride's peace of mind.

> **BE PREPARED TO**
>
> Locate the parents, but if they are unavailable, attempt to get the child under control without creating an unpleasant spectacle. Avoid disciplining the kid, unless you are prepared to incur the wrath of the parents, or, worse, baby-sit for the night.

The Elephant in the Room

Every single person in the bride's and groom's collected families studiously ignores the antics of the attending alcoholic, who everyone hoped desperately would behave but who is progressively becoming more obnoxious and drunk.

> **BE PREPARED TO**
>
> Follow suit and ignore the situation or, in an emergency, such as a buffet table about to be toppled, take action.

The Academy Awards

A rather inebriated guest starts making a speech and won't stop, or makes one speech then keeps returning to the microphone repeatedly to say what he or she "forgot" the first time around.

⊰ BE PREPARED TO ⊱

Cringe but stay in your seat—and pray the bride and groom designated an MC. If the speaker really gets out of control, consider going up to wait in line to make another speech yourself, and hope the pressure of your presence convinces the speaker to give up.

The West Side Story

Sometimes, the bride's and groom's families act like opposing gangs for reasons that don't seem very logical. They might be feuding over something as broad as religious differences, or as specific as how the guest list was divided—but the tension is thicker than the buttercream frosting on the wedding cake.

⊰ BE PREPARED TO ⊱

Act as you would in the case of an After-School Special situation.

WORD ALERT

⊰ THE TOPPER ⊱

This word is sometimes used to describe something that puts a cap on a situation, such as, "It's bad enough that I was singing the *Flashdance* soundtrack in public, but imitating Jennifer Beals dancing—now that's the topper!" At weddings, however, the term refers to the miniature bride-and-groom figurine that goes on the wedding cake.

USAGE: The bride says, "We paid the caterer four hundred bucks to find us that fabulous vintage topper."

CORRECT RESPONSE: "Now that's the topper."

THE END OF THE RECEPTION

After the ceremonial cutting of the wedding cake, where the bride and groom feed each other, the bride gathers her bridesmaids for the bouquet toss. This usually signals the end of the reception, and it occurs just before the bride and groom depart to change for their honeymoon. Knowing how to handle the bouquet toss and your other final duties is key to concluding the wedding in fabulous bridesmaid style.

BOUQUET TOSS

The days when bridesmaids and other single female guests shoved each other out of the way to be the lucky one to catch the flowers—the sign that they would be married next—are disappearing fast. Whether the bouquet-toss backlash is happening because single women are loath to draw attention to their dateless status, are currently dating someone they have no interest in marrying, or enjoy being single too much to jinx their luck, the toss inspires less fervor now than it did in the days when single women over thirty were called spinsters. No matter what your feelings are on the issue, however, every unmarried bridesmaid should participate in the toss. Get into it! And, if the bouquet comes toward you, *do not run away*.

If a garter toss is going to take place, it will happen right after the bouquet toss. The groom tosses the bride's garter to the bachelors (he might remove it from the bride's leg directly beforehand, in front of the crowd). According to tradition, the man who catches it will be the next to get married. At some weddings, the man who catches the garter is asked to put it on the leg of the woman who catches the bouquet. This situation has potential to become a completely embarrassing disaster for everyone involved, but you never know— if sparks fly between the two, a romance might take root.

GOOD-BYE TOKENS

At the chosen time, the maid of honor and bridesmaids should get their supply of rose petals, rice, or sparklers—and distribute them to all the guests—so that when the newlyweds leave the reception, the guests can say good-bye and shower them with good-luck tokens. If the newlyweds are leaving for their honeymoon directly from the reception, the bridesmaids might accompany the bride in the dressing room while she changes into traveling clothes, and then perform the good-bye ritual when the couple is prepared to depart.

THE POST-RECEPTION PARTY

In the old days, the end of the reception was the end of wedding—but with today's longer "wedding weekends," this is rarely the case. The caterers have packed up and the lights in the reception hall have been dimmed, but this doesn't mean the festivities are over.

Increasingly, the newlyweds don't want the party to stop! Instead of leaving for their honeymoon or adjourning to their wedding-night hotel suite directly after the reception, many couples are choosing to celebrate with friends once the evening is officially over and the older folks have gone to bed.

The idea of a post-reception party isn't entirely new. Traditionally, such events were arranged to entertain guests after weddings that had finished early in the day; they provided an opportunity for the bride's mother to spend additional time with her out-of-town guests and perhaps serve them dinner if a full meal was not offered at the early reception. The genteel origins of the party have little in common with the new incarnation of post-reception festivities, which generally involve cocktails and late-night mingling.

These days, the post-reception party takes place in a hotel suite rented by a group of bridesmaids or ushers—often the same hotel where the bride and groom will be spending the night—or at a private home if one is available. Occasionally, the event will be held at a nearby bar that is open late into the night. The only drawback to this alternative is that at the end of the night, sober drivers can be hard to find! This is why having the party at a hotel makes so much sense.

As a maid of honor or bridesmaid, you might offer to host the event—but only if drinking cocktails and chatting until dawn is your cup of tea. The party often happens even if the bride and groom decline to attend, since it provides an opportunity for young, energetic guests to talk over the ceremony, blow off steam, and continue having fun! By no means are you *required* to host or attend a post-reception party, although if the bride and groom will be stopping by, you will no doubt want to be there so you can wish them well one more time.

AFTERGLOW

Due to the increasingly popular custom of the delayed honeymoon, newlyweds often stick around the day after the wedding for an event that includes close family, the wedding party, and other guests who are flying out late in the day. Late-morning brunches, afternoon picnics, and beach barbecues are popular. Traditionally, such occasions have been organized by the bride's mother, but these days, anyone with the inclination or means may host the event. After a spring wedding, a backyard might be a lovely setting for a casual morning event to send friends and family of the couple off in style. If you choose to take charge, send out invitations early so folks can plan in advance. If hosting an event is the last thing on your mind—with the possible exception of a burn-your-bridesmaid-dress party—simply show up at the afterglow with a smile on your face.

TEN FABULOUS WAYS TO INDULGE
THE BRIDE AFTER THE WEDDING

1 Make a grand gesture to celebrate the couple's commitment by planting a tree in their backyard the night before or after the wedding. (Run your idea by the bride or groom first, and don't dig up the roses by mistake!)

2 Collect the disposable cameras from the reception tables and develop the film. Often, the professional photographs aren't available for months, and the newlyweds will love returning home from their honeymoon to find piles of fun wedding snapshots.

3 Before the bride leaves the reception, give her a honeymoon kit stuffed with sunscreen, sunglasses, a great book for the plane, and a blank journal in which to record her adventures. Toss in those hilarious Polaroids you took at the rehearsal dinner.

4 Organize an intimate post-reception gathering where everyone can kick off their shoes and toast the newlyweds one more time before hitting the hay.

5 Leave a basket of treats on their dining room table the night before they return from their trip, to cushion their return to reality. If you've forgotten to get their keys, leave a pretty bouquet and a "Welcome Home" card on their doorstep.

6 Several months after the wedding, organize a girls' night to revisit the bridal shower scrapbook (see page 76), pore over the wedding photographs, and reminisce about all the fun!

7 Schedule a group manicure and pedicure with the girls to help her stave off the inevitable post-wedding depression after she gets back from the honeymoon.

9 Offer to be the bride's "special helper" at the reception after she and the groom depart, and collect the cake topper, the top tier of the wedding cake, the guest book, extra flowers, and the gifts, and transport them to a designated place. The best man or the bride's father will be in charge of tipping the musicians and caterers, but you should add your enthusiastic thanks.

8 Give the couple theater, ballet, or concert tickets for an evening about a month after the wedding. This gives the couple a chance to dress up and go out on a date while they are still broke from the wedding, overwhelmed with unpacking, and starting back at work.

10 If the couple isn't leaving for their honeymoon immediately, decorate their bedroom or hotel room. They'll be thrilled after the long wedding day to find their wedding-night chamber filled with a chilled bottle of champagne, fragrant flowers, a book of love poems, and a small portable stereo playing their favorite music.

TEN FABULOUS WAYS TO REVIVE
YOURSELF AFTER BEING A BRIDESMAID

1 Host a bad-bridesmaid-dress fashion show—at home, behind closed doors, with no married friends invited. The guest who wears the most unflattering bridesmaid dress, and has the pictures to prove she wore it in public, wins a gift! (Have everyone chip in ten bucks for a gift certificate to a salon, so the lucky winner can have the beauty that she deserves.)

2 Put your bridesmaid training on your resume and use your new skills to start a fabulous new career.

WHAT YOU LOVED ABOUT BEING A BRIDESMAID	YOUR NEW CAREER
Getting to know people	Therapist
Spending money without guilt	Politician
Public speaking	Politician
Partying	Politician
Making everything go smoothly	Event planner
Constant emotional drama	Television scriptwriter

3 Claim your bridesmaid expenses as tax deductions. (Check with an accountant first, and be sure you have convincing proof that you did professional networking related to your business.)

4 Treat yourself to some lovely aromatherapy candles, fabulous new silky pajamas, and an afternoon massage. Why should you only overspend on other people?

5 Use scissors to cut up the dress for future use. A taffeta skirt makes excellent packing material for china, wineglasses, or other delicate items when you move, for example, and absorbent bodice material works beautifully for household chores.

6 Really despising the dress gives it bad voodoo power. Send the thing to your evil ex-boss or jerky ex-boyfriend anonymously. They won't know who sent it or why they have received it, but it will definitely creep them out, especially if you toss in a copy of Stephen King's *Carrie* with the promlike dress.

7 Start a company that designs bridesmaid dresses that are actually flattering, and watch your net worth soar.

8 Use your bridesmaid experience as a cocktail-party conversation starter. You'll be amazed at how the shyest wallflowers or deafest old folks will perk up when this topic arises. When you feel really confident with your material, consider taking your story to the airwaves on a television talk show!

9 Write a book about your bridesmaid experience.

10 Schedule celebratory drinks with the bride—well, she's not really a bride anymore, is she?— and tell her how delighted you are to have her joining you back on earth.